SCHOLARSHIP
Pursuit

THE HOW TO GUIDE
FOR WINNING COLLEGE SCHOLARSHIPS

S. Y. Koot

With Dr. Arthur L. Jue and Corine Neumiller

1st WORLD
PUBLISHING

Scholarship Pursuit

THE HOW TO GUIDE FOR WINNING COLLEGE SCHOLARSHIPS

S. Y. Koot

With Dr. Arthur L. Jue and Corine Neumiller

Copyright © 1996, 2007 by S. Y. Koot, Arthur L. Jue, and Corine Neumiller

Published by 1stWorld Publishing
1100 North 4th St. Suite 131, Fairfield, Iowa 52556
tel: 641-209-5000 • fax: 641-209-3001
web: www.1stworldpublishing.com

First Edition

LCCN: 2007931787

SoftCover ISBN: 978-1-4218-9801-8

HardCover ISBN: 978-1-4218-9802-5

eBook ISBN: 978-1-4218-9803-2

To every scholarshipper with the desire
and determination to achieve and succeed,
may you find happiness and fulfilment in a bright future.

PREFACE

A Letter to the Student

Dear Student,

Hello and welcome aboard! This is certainly an exciting moment in your life as you begin to apply for scholarships and anticipate your future in college! We hope to share with you the practical system that my family and I have developed after years of personal experiences and many thousands of dollars in scholarship awards and honors. More importantly, we hope to teach you the "thought patterns" upon which to build successful experiences in this competitive arena.

No matter which high school you presently attend or which university you plan to enter, your key to securing college scholarships ultimately hinges on learning, remembering, and applying some simple, yet profound, principles of success detailed in this workbook.

Our course is unique because it expressly teaches you how to qualify for and win scholarships by revealing, step-by-step, a method to use once you have actually obtained the scholarship application. Due dates, requirements, and addresses may change, but the winning principles described in this kit are timeless!

We know it works, and we know that you can do it! Best wishes for every future success!

Happy scholarshipping!

A Letter to the Parent(s)

Dear Parent(s)

This must be a thrilling time for you, as you and your child share in the excitement of what possibilities the future holds. But if you're like most concerned parents, you are probably feeling somewhat anxious as you anticipate all the financial obligations that will accompany a college education.

As the mother of four children, all of whom attained college educations, I understand your anxiety. It is, therefore, our sincere goal throughout the following pages to explain in simple, but detailed, terms the realities involved in obtaining scholarships for a college education and to provide your son(s) and/or daughter(s) with the proper tools in order to build a solid financial foundation for obtaining higher education.

Because your parental role is crucial and can make all the difference to your child's success in learning how to qualify for and win scholarships, we have included a special chapter just for you.

Having been through numerous successes with my children (sprinkled with hard trial and error), I know what a fruitful and fulfilling experience "scholarshipping" can be, and my family and I are confident that it will be the same for you and yours!

May your invaluable parental contributions be perpetually manifested in the sum total of your students' successes!

Warmest regards,

TABLE OF CONTENTS

INTRODUCTION

1

A ship in the harbor is safe, but that is NOT what ships are for.

John Shedd

INTRODUCTION

 Our approach to developing this course stems from the ancient Confucian philosophy,

"If you GIVE a man a fish,
You feed him for a day.
If you TEACH a man to fish,
You feed him for life."

Finding the "fish" or scholarship is the easy part. A wealth of unclaimed scholarships exist, and there are a myriad of ways to locate them. Unfortunately, however, when it comes to teaching you how to actually "catch the fish," or how to win scholarships, often very little information currently available truly proves useful. Rather than being just another list of scholarship sources with names and addresses or a manual on need-based financial aid (loans or grants), this course expressly teaches you how to qualify for and win scholarships once you have actually obtained the scholarship applications. The thoughts and information provided here are based on proven experiences as well as "lessons learned" by past top scholarship winners.

DEFINITION

"Scholarship"

Monetary gifts awarded in recognition of your own personal merit and individual achievement as opposed to other need-based financial aid, grants or loans.

COURSE CONTENTS

With the application in hand, your ability to win scholarships depends primarily upon how effective you are in communicating your personal qualities and accomplishments. Scholarship winners use a number of basic principles and skills. These include:

- Becoming involved in school and community activities
- Recording personal accomplishments
- Acquiring letters of recommendations
- Writing persuasive essays
- Mastering powerful interviewing skills
- Developing proficiency in communicating both verbally and non-verbally
- Asserting confidence
- And much more.

This scholarship guide will explain these principles and skills in the following chapters and give you the opportunity to learn and practice them. We encourage you to use the sample application (see **Appendix B**), practice questions, and worksheets provided. In addition, we hope that you will use this system to keep your scholarship information organized in one place so that you can save precious time finding what you need when you need it the most.

H I G H L I G H T

"Lessons Learned"

At the opening of the scholarship season for high school seniors, a Junior one day announced that he intended to enter college a year early and simultaneously complete his high school Senior year during his college Freshman year. That announcement, alone, was surprising enough to his parents, until he also decided at this "11th hour" to compete for Senior-level scholarships.

Panic? Not in the least—because all the essential information had already been *organized* according to the system that was contained in THIS kit! All that this student really had to do was complete the scholarship applications and customize his personal portfolio to satisfy each particular scholarship's criteria.

HOW IS THE COURSE ORGANIZED?

Each chapter is organized to take you through the entire scholarship process **step-by-step** from filling out the application form to facing a panel of interview judges. The contents of this course are also written as succinctly as possible in short paragraphs—including true-story highlights and definitions —to afford easy topical reference and to allow maximum storage space for all of the scholarship materials that you will soon be acquiring.

Notice that each page contains an empty column next to the text so that you can immediately scribble down any notes and thoughts that come freely to your mind. In short, we hope that this binder will become the literal tap-root of your scholarship success!

HOW TO EFFECTIVELY USE THIS COURSE

In order to become familiar with the course as quickly as possible, thereby giving yourself a competitive edge, here is an effective method of study that we affectionately call *The Picnic Approach.*

Retire to your own secluded hideaway during the early morning or any other time you feel most attentive to inspiration. If you do not have a favorite spot, simply take your "picnic basket" and GO. Find any *quiet,* agreeable place where you can be alone, undisturbed, and undistracted.

You may end up in your own bedroom or in the nearby mountains or even in the library, but wherever you are, the surrounding environment must be conducive to creativity—a place where you can truly concentrate and *think.* Next, read each page of this book, cover to cover, in the following sequence:

THE PICNIC APPROACH

Step 1

✎ **INSPECT** the overall contents of the book. Quickly browse through the major sections, looking at headings as well as highlighted areas. Get a general feel for the outline. This step prepares your mind to better receive, process, and organize the information.

Step 2

✎ **QUESTION** while you read. Ask yourself how the material applies to your own circumstance. Think of specific questions in order to create a greater desire to know the answer. As a result, your ability to concentrate and persist in reading this material will increase.

Step 3

✎ **READ** to understand. Study each principle carefully, and read from beginning to end. Take notes in the opposite space provided.

Step 4

✐ **APPLY** the principles you learn by completing the exercise worksheets provided and by working on your own scholarship applications. The difference between the winner and the "also ran" is active participation, not merely passive learning.

Step 5

✐ **REVIEW** the reading material OFTEN. By so doing, your memory will be refreshed, your insights will be broadened, and you will be able to continually enhance your application style as well as sharpen your overall scholarship savvy.

Read this course as if you had been asked to teach a class or to write a paper on it. This approach will not only improve your power to absorb a wealth of information but also enhance your ability to integrate these very same principles in your "scholarshipping" efforts.

ONE LAST NOTE

The examples, formats, and worksheets in each chapter are quality benchmarks developed from the experiences of other top scholars. They are provided for you to use in developing, evaluating, critiquing, and measuring your overall presentation style. However, they are not concrete, fixed patterns to which you must strictly adhere. Maintain high standards of consistent quality in every application, but be equally creative by tailoring each response to your own situation. Stay uniquely YOU!

T H O U G H T

CHARACTER...is like a tree and reputation like its shadow. The shadow is what we think of it; the tree is the real thing.

—*Abraham Lincoln*

Your own personality and character should shine through all of your scholarship applications, materials, and interviews so that you always stand out as the interesting and exceptionally capable individual that you are.

Remember, the benefits of the scholarship process rest not only in the award itself, but also in the personal contentment derived from having numerous growth opportunities and from knowing where you stand not just in your own school, but among students and schools throughout your county, other cities, the nation, and even the world. Happy scholarshipping!

PREPARE FOR SUCCESS

2

I **will** PrePare myself, then, when my opportunity comes

I will be ready.

Abraham Lincoln

CONTENTS
○○○○○○○○○○○○○○○○○○

PREPARE FOR SUCCESS!

Basic preparations, Getting started, Becoming active!

A young man hiking in the desert once desired, above all else, to capture a snake. So, he clambered up a large rock with a great, big steel tub, waited patiently for some time, and then, "CLUNK," dropped the tub over the first slithering snake that meandered his way. Then the young man jumped down from the rock and sat on the tub while contemplating what he should do next!

Like most worthwhile endeavors, preparing for success as you pursue your own "snakes" in life takes good planning and preparation. Yet, we have seen students who far too often, like our desert hiker, fail to realize what kind of necessary preparations are involved in order to win scholarships. Even worse, students fall short of believing they can qualify for and win scholarships and end up letting golden opportunities slip quietly by.

BUT, the right kind of thinking is to *make* yourself qualify by working steadfastly and planning as *early* as you possibly can. Constant preparation is the great secret of success that all high achievers must learn to apply.

Consider, for instance, trying to cook a gourmet meal without first purchasing the necessary raw materials, or erecting a beautiful mansion before laying a proper foundation. The Boy Scout motto is "be prepared." Likewise, scholarship winners plan the details carefully. Before executing competitive strategies of their own, these achievers simply start investing time and energy in *preparing* themselves by becoming involved in various activities, serving others, and acquiring a broad range of skills, from strong leadership to effective communication abilities. Consequently, when the time approaches for them to compete for scholarships, they confidently engender the kind of portfolio that easily distinguishes them from the rest of the crowd. Once you have made such an investment of time, yourself, we are confident that you, too, will feel the effects of significant rewards.

This chapter explains in detail the fundamental secrets of scholarship *preparation* and provides you with a general checklist of "things to do" in helping yourself become prepared. We recommend that you start preparing in your freshman year of high school—if not earlier. But regardless of your current year in school, the key is to start preparing *today*! You've taken the first step by reading this guide. Now, as you apply the principles within, let us help you the rest of the way.

T H O U G H T

IF you take
　　the time to be prepared,...
　　　　...you'll never be
　　　　　　taken by surprise.

ASSESSING YOUR GOALS

Take a few moments right now to identify some of your personal expectations, feelings, strengths, weaknesses, and apprehensions that you associate with the scholarshipping process. It is essential for you to not only realistically acknowledge and capitalize on your personal strengths, but to make any major areas of weakness irrelevant. Perhaps facing an interview intimidates you or focusing on your extra-curricular activities holds the most potential for improvement. Once you recognize these personal areas of challenge, verbalize and organize them into clear, specific, practical *goals*, and *immediately* write them down.

For example, as mentioned above, if you are intimidated at the thought of interviews, then make it a goal to master 90% of the practice interview questions contained in this workbook. If you are unsure about how to represent all of your activities in a scholarship application, make it your goal to read the particular chapter in this workbook on applications three times—or at least until all the mysteries have been taken out of scholarshipping. By making specific and measurable goals, not only will you be changing weaknesses into strengths, but you will also be monitoring your actual progress towards success as you become more confident and assured in your ability to qualify for scholarships.

To give you a "quick start," included here is a shortened version of the worksheet about goals and visions found in Chapter 7. It is entitled "My Personal Progress Goals" and is an effective tool that can become a focusing and empowering force in your effort to pursue scholarships. Take a moment now to reflect upon your personal mission, goals, barriers, and desires (see Chapter 7). First, think about your mission on a personal level, then think of how you are going to change the world!

Of course, recording your vision is just the first step. If left uncultivated, visions can become blocked. How? By wrong attitudes, for example, when you start saying to yourself, "What's the use?" or when someone else belittles or ridicules your vision.

Personal visions can become unblocked by dreaming and imagining what could happen in the future and by reminding yourself of your individual worth as reflected in your vision and mission statement documented below. When the going gets tough, look at what you wrote on the following page. This can help you to stay focused and to remember both your written goals as well as the reason behind why you desired to obtain scholarships for college in the first place.

MISSION STATEMENT FORMULA:

I want to_____in a way which_____so that _____as measured by_____.

Now, record these thoughts in the following spaces:

MY PERSONAL PROGRESS GOALS:

MISSION STATEMENT

_____

_____

_____

LONG RANGE GOALS

_____

_____

_____

SHORT-TERM ACTION GOALS

1. _____
2. _____
3. _____

POTENTIAL BARRIERS   AREAS TO EMPHASIZE

_____   _____

_____   _____

_____   _____

WHAT I WANT TO ACCOMPLISH FROM THIS COURSE

_____

_____

_____

TALK WITH YOUR PARENTS

Preparing for scholarships is an opportune time to talk seriously with your parents about your goals and dreams, about what's important to you in order to succeed in high school, about choosing a college that will help you realize your potential, and about your personal preparations for winning scholarships. Give it a try!

Your parents may or may not be inclined to impart much

assistance to you in your scholarship pursuit, but most likely, if they are willing, you'll be amazed at how much advice and wisdom lay hidden in the recesses of your parents' life experiences, and perhaps more importantly, you will have gained their invaluable support. Constantly keep this line of communication open as best as you can, and frequently "update" your parents on the status of the goals that you have made.

MEET WITH YOUR COUNSELOR

Consult with your high school counselor(s) as early as your Freshman year and as frequently as possible thereafter. Remind the counselor(s) of your intentions to apply for scholarships, so that when scholarship announcements arrive at the office, your name comes to mind immediately. Counselors can be extremely instrumental in helping you plan the kind of academic course work that both qualifies you for college entrance and also enables you to compete successfully for scholarships.

Unfortunately, due to the current educational environment of budget and funding constraints throughout the country, many schools have limited counseling resources or must tolerate high student-counselor ratios. Therefore, it is all the more important for *you* to focus on building a good relationship with your counselor(s), helping them to remember you, and discovering other ways to tap into the scholarshipping resources available at your school.

SELECT APPROPRIATE ACADEMIC CLASSES

Select your academic classes with college in mind. Try taking as many honors and advanced placement classes as you can reasonably handle. However, no matter what curriculum you pursue, always remember that it is equally important for you to enjoy what you are learning and to perform *well*. We don't mean that every class should be an honors course, nor all too easy. Achieving **balance** and the appropriate level of **challenge** are the key concepts. For example, one "straight A" student was rejected by her first choice college because she took all fun, but non-essential, classes. Look inside yourself and discuss with your family the curriculum that best fulfills your personal needs and future goals.

It has been our experience that what academic scholarship panels (and college admission boards) generally prefer are students who have demonstrated their motivation by consistently earning good grades throughout all four years of high school and who have usually gone on to choose some more advanced courses in a particular subject, rather than just stopping after all the basic graduation requirements are met. If you have studied a foreign language for two years, continue on and take an advanced course, or if you have completed basic Freshman Science and Biology, take Chemistry, Physics, and/or Anatomy. Following through with advanced courses reflects your self motivation. It is important to evince both the depth and breadth of your educational experience when scholarshipping.

Maintaining high academic standards of excellence is just as important whether you are concentrating on sports or leadership-oriented scholarships. No matter what type of scholarship you pursue, round out your education with a balanced mix of coursework.

MAINTAIN A GOOD GPA

We often hear students lamenting with each other, "There is noooo way I could ever win a scholarship—I don't have anywhere near a 4.0." Good news: Not all scholarship winners have earned perfect 4.0's either. They just did their best to maintain a good GPA and then qualified for competition by meeting the scholarship's minimum Grade Point Average criteria.

For many scholarships, minimum GPA requirements probably range between 3.2 and 3.5. Some requirements are set lower and some are set higher. If your grades are less than what you would consider as "qualifying" material, begin now to work just a little harder. Remember that while having a 4.0+ GPA on an application is always a bonus, it is usually far from being the sole criteria for determining a winner. Winners are those applicants who not only excel in the classroom but perform well in areas that are just as important in the development of a well-rounded individual. They are individuals with leadership responsibilities, community service, and athletic involvement, for example.

GET A SOCIAL SECURITY NUMBER

If you haven't already done so, be sure to obtain a social security number. A social security number may be requested by some applications for tracking purposes. Chances are that you have been carrying one for sometime, but just in case, here is the telephone number and website address of the Social Security Administration:

Social Security Administration

1-800-772-1213

http://www.ssa.gov

When calling this number or searching the website, ask for or find the Social Security Administration office nearest to your current home location. You may have to supply your zip code, after which the closest location to your home will be identified. Once you have obtained your social security number, try to memorize it. Although the use of social security numbers is decreasing due to privacy concerns, you may need it during this process. In either case, it will be constantly used throughout your life on many important documents besides scholarship applications.

REGISTER FOR AND TAKE THE REQUIRED COLLEGE ENTRANCE EXAMS

You will be frequently asked to submit one or more scores from the following standardized college entrance exams: PSAT, SAT, and/or ACT (see definition box). These tests are usually taken in your Senior year; however, once you are in high school, you can begin ANYTIME taking these tests.

Check with your counselor to obtain your registration packet which includes the published bulletin of SAT and ACT test dates. If you are unsatisfied with a particular score, you can retake the tests—they are offered several times a year.

We suggest obtaining test preparation workbooks and spending a little time on them every day. Some individuals find it advantageous to repeat these tests, receiving higher test scores the second and third time around. However, you must pay the registration fee each time you take the test, which may prove quite costly. Trade-offs also exist between taking multiple standardized tests and spending time on other classroom and extracurricular activities.

Incidentally, when registering for these tests, you have the option of sending copies of your test score to a few colleges or scholarship programs of your choice. Should you choose this option, realize that when your scores are forwarded, they can affect your chances of being considered for scholarships and/or admission at the receiving institutions.

So, if you can confidently anticipate desirable results, or if you feel that you will not be able to retake the test, by all means, take advantage of this option, especially since copies for the first few institutions are generally free of charge. If you are less certain about the test outcome, or if you can afford to retake the test, then you may benefit from waiting until your score has been determined (*after* taking the test) before deciding whether to send it to any particular institution.

Although there may be additional costs for sending the scores after the test is taken (as opposed to the free offer during test registration), for many students, the benefits of ensuring a good "first impression" and examining actual scores before they are sent seem to justify the additional cost. In either case, remember that your test scores are usually just one of many criteria used in determining the winners of scholarships offered by colleges and other groups.

One test that should be of particular interest to you is the PSAT, a preliminary, national test administered ONCE annually and geared towards preparing Juniors for the SAT. However, *you **do not** have to be a Junior to register for this test.* Therefore, if you have the opportunity to take this test before your Junior year, do it for the experience. Use it to evaluate your current scholastic preparedness and become familiar with the test itself. Note that the score received in your Junior year is the only score that is regarded as official by the program even if you received a higher score as a Freshman or a

Sophomore. Some individuals regard the PSAT as even more important than the SAT since it is the basis for determining the distinguished National Merit Scholarship Awards.

Again, like the GPA, remember that these scores are not the sole measure of your success. Some scholarships, such as the National Merit Scholarship Program or certain other prestigious university scholarships, are likely to place more emphasis on having a high test score for preliminary screening purposes. Others may weigh these scores together with other factors such as your GPA, rank in class, activities, leadership, etc.

DEFINITION

"Standardized Tests"

Although these tests change from time to time, here is how they are currently structured (as of the printing of this workbook):

PSAT: PRE SCHOLASTIC APTITUDE TEST

The PSAT is a crucial qualifying exam for the National Merit Scholarship Program sponsored by the National Merit Scholarship Corporation. It is given once a year, usually in the later part of the year and consists of 3 sections: mathematics, critical reading, and writing. The test takes a little over two hours to complete. Scores range from 20 to 80 (high) on each section. There are several PSAT test preparation booklets available in your local bookstore.

SAT: SCHOLASTIC APTITUDE TEST

This test is administered by the Educational Testing Service in:

Princeton, NJ 609/771-7600 (8:30am-9:30pm EST)
Berkeley, CA 510/849-0950 (8:15am-4:30pm PST)
http://www.ets.org

The SAT is divided into two portions, SAT I and SAT II. Most colleges and scholarships require the SAT I portion. SAT I focuses on reasoning skills in the verbal and math categories. SAT II tests specific subjects such as English literature, American history, Chemistry, French, etc.

The Verbal SAT I portion asks primarily critical reading questions (selections from the Humanities, Social Sciences, Natural Sciences, and fiction/non-fiction) as well as sentence completions (fill-in-the-blanks). The Math SAT I section focuses mostly on multiple choice questions. There is also a writing section, which includes multiple choice and student-produced essay responses. Each section is scored between 200 and 800 (highest). Some test strategists argue that if you can eliminate some choices, it is generally regarded as advantageous to guess. However, there is a penalty for guessing incorrectly. The SAT has come under increasing criticism for testing biases, and some colleges are considering dropping it as a requirement. So, be sure to check whether the test is a requirement for your scholarship application and/or college entrance application.

ACT: AMERICAN COLLEGE TEST ASSESSMENT

This test is administered by American College Testing in Iowa City:

ACT Registration, PO Box 414,
Iowa City, Iowa 52243 (319)337-1270
http://www.act.org/aap/

The ACT consists of a battery of 4 sections with the following number and types of questions: 75 English, 60 Mathematics, 40 Reading and 40 Science Reasoning. There is also an optional writing test. For the ACT, you receive a composite score which represents an average of the 4 test scores. The range is from 1 to 36 (maximum). On certain test dates, you can also receive a copy of the test you took. For this test, it is generally better to guess when uncertain—there are no penalties for wrong answers.

While the SAT is often purported to test a student's innate ability, the ACT is generally regarded as testing what a student has learned to date in their educational experience. Some have argued that the questions on the ACT are more straightforward and less ambiguous than the SAT. However, for our purposes, it would be wise to take both the SAT and ACT so that you are prepared for whatever a scholarship application may require.

BECOME KNOWN AND ACTIVE IN YOUR SCHOOL AND COMMUNITY

Become involved! The importance of this single aspect cannot be overemphasized. When the sum of your efforts and contributions have been channeled into bettering aspects of the school, community, or world in which you live, you will not only foster a deeper feeling of satisfaction associated with selfless service, but also be deserving of the merit and recognition that comes with the honor of a scholarship.

Making that difference can only be achieved by earnestly *doing* something. So, be proactive! Participate in school and community activities. Join clubs that your department offers. Run for offices in the student body council or your favorite clubs (even though there may be limited offices available, you can still be very active). Volunteer to chair a project. Take risks and put your "neck on the line"! If you have special talents or skills, offer to share them. Become known by serving and benefiting your school and community. In other words, whatever you enjoy doing, just go for it and become involved!

H I G H L I G H T

"Making a Difference"

One creative student excelled in emergency preparedness techniques and lifesaving skills. Wishing to share his knowledge and talent with others for the benefit of the community, he talked to his Anatomy/ Physiology teacher and a short while later, had planned, organized, and implemented a week-long CPR Certification Course for his school's entire Anatomy/Physiology Department. In just one short week, over 200 students and faculty were certified in CPR! In fact, this student's "little" idea became a permanent implementation in the school's curriculum. Even after this young man graduated, countless students have continued to become certified in CPR each year through the course that he established. Some students have actually used CPR to save lives!

As you allow your level of school and community involvement to grow throughout your high school career, we are confident that many more windows of opportunities will become opened to you. When the time approaches to gather letters of recommendation, or when the school is seeking promising students to involve in special tasks (and especially in scholarship competitions!), your reputation as a "stellar" individual may be the deciding factor. Furthermore, many scholarship committees regard your level of involvement and your sustained commitment during high school as a measure of your future impact to your chosen college, and more importantly, beyond the university environment as a contributing member of society.

RUN FOR LEADERSHIP POSITIONS

A wise millionaire once stated that becoming part of the wealthy 5% elite in America is easy because, although 99% of the population says that it wants to be rich, only 1% of the people are willing to put in the energy and effort to get there. So, in effect, you are competing with a very small segment of the entire population. The same principle holds true for leadership. While everyone wants to be (and is capable of becoming) a leader, most people remain followers, because very few of us are willing to make the personal investments necessary or take the risks required to become great leaders.

Universities and colleges (not to mention society in general) desire to recruit individuals who have leadership potential— students who deserve to be developed and who can serve as role models in the community, thereby building a reputation for and bringing honor to the university and community at large. Therefore, leadership is one of the most important aspects that you can exhibit in your quest to obtain scholarships and enter the college of your preference.

As you serve and lead, be sure you also involve others in the planning and decision-making process. This kind of people-oriented leadership requires developing a steady balance of patience, diplomacy, flexibility, initiative, and humor. Rest assured that as you strive to include others in important leadership decisions, they are likely to become more cooperative and supportive of your goals, as well as become more willing to put forth greater personal effort in accomplishing the tasks at hand. Speaking from personal experience, one prominent student leader also said, "Leadership is a great way to network." You never know whom you'll meet or whom you'll help or which hidden talents of yours will emerge to get you through challenges!

HIGHLIGHT

"The Winning Opportunity"

A movie star once commented that the secret of success is to "show up." In many cases, some of the leadership opportunities that many students have enjoyed during their high school years, have occurred simply because they took the time to show up where other students opted to stay home, hang out, or simply do nothing. For example, one young man became the President of his High School Freshman Class just because he was on the ball. During the first few weeks of school, while all of the other Freshmen were busy finding their classrooms and becoming accustomed to a strange environment and new teachers, he asked an administrator how to run for the position and the deadline to apply. He was the only candidate to apply because no other Freshman thought about it (at least until it was too late to apply!).

Contrary to popular belief, exhibiting leadership does not always necessarily involve loud, extroverted, commanding, "rally-the-troops" kind of behaviors we tend to glorify in society. Although these types of leaders are more easily identified and lauded, many of the world's greatest leaders have been in reality quiet, unobtrusive individuals possessing strong characteristics of *understanding* and *empathy*. They lead by *example* and were great followers as well as great leaders.

What all great leaders have in common is an unwavering

sense of mission and a vision of what could exist but that does not at the present time. Many leaders are agents of change and innovation. They are willing to take the risks necessary to see their visions through to fruition.

Assert your leadership by serving at the forefront as the president of a club, chairperson of a committee, or founder of an organization. Remember, however, that leadership skills can also be exhibited in the types of contributions that you make to facilitate events through small actions and activities as well as the large,grandiose efforts. A willingness or talent for listening can be just as effective a leadership attribute as the ability to rouse an audience through great orations and speeches.

Furthermore, in the community where you live, a plethora of opportunities probably exist for you to serve, become involved, and develop your leadership potential through non-profit volunteer organizations, charitable causes, and civic or governmental agencies. You won't have to look very hard to find something that interests you and to which you can contribute significantly. In fact, most community service-related organizations are usually "desperate" for talented individuals who are willing to go the extra mile and participate. Besides the personal satisfaction you gain through community involvement, your chances for networking will increase, and your probability of earning scholarships will multiply tremendously!

In addition to running for leadership positions at school or in your community, leadership can and should be demonstrated within the confines of your own home. Many scholarship organizations are beginning to ask more frequently about contributions in the home environment as well as the outside community in order to ascertain whether an individual has been able to maintain that critical balance between home, school, and community. This ability to balance priorities is a skill necessary for young leaders to truly stay successful in the long run. Many great leaders have commented that few other achievements in their lives have been as satisfying as the success achieved in their own homes.

HIGHLIGHT

"The Youth Commissioner"

During a heavy period of tests and exams, an announcement was made to Juniors at a particular high school about the availability of applications to join a "Youth Commission." The application form looked very unattractive and unprofessional. Moreover, it failed to offer any explanation about what a "Youth Commission" was or did. Although the form seemed discouraging, one self-initiated young man picked up the application and called a phone number listed on it to ask more questions.

The young man was extremely busy with his school work and other activities, but he applied for the position and was selected. Much to his surprise, he discovered that members of this "Youth Commission" were screened by the city council and were appointed by the Mayor to act on behalf of all city youth in recommending legislation and working on city-wide youth projects. Whereas he might have opted not to submit this application because of his heavy schedule or the form's "unfamiliar" appearance, this student ACTED and gained a valuable experience through his service on the commission. Not only did he become a friend of the Mayor, but he also opened many more doors for himself in providing local community activism.

Moreover, one of the city council members later served on the panel of a particular scholarship for which he was applying. Needless to say, he won the award!

THE SCHOLARSHIP SEARCH

Although the objective of this kit is *not* to offer a list of scholarships for which you can apply (but rather to arm you with the knowledge of *how* to apply *successfully*), we would like to direct you to some places where you can find a number of scholarships and sources for college financing. Besides visiting your own school counselor, counseling office, or career center, many teachers often independently announce scholarship opportunities that come their way, and many organizations offer scholarship opportunities through your local district office or via the Internet. Sometimes it pays to visit other high school campuses in person or visit them online to see what their bulletin boards have to offer. Also, ask if your parent's company offers scholarships specifically for children of employees. The university that you plan to attend usually provides a myriad of scholarships as well.

If you have a community library nearby, visit it and look in the card or online catalog under "scholarships". You may also have to look under "grants", as many organizations lump scholarships and grants together in the same category of publications. You will be surprised at what you find! Also, if you have a local university or community college nearby—even one that you do not plan on attending—visit its library or website as a source of scholarship leads as well. If you visit a library in person, be sure to search through the "For Reference Use Only" section, too (and bring plenty of change to make copies!). In conducting the research for this kit, we have literally found volumes filled with thousands of scholarship sources, addresses, information, and leads simply by visiting local libraries and searching online. We've listed a few in **Appendix A** at the end of this workbook. Sources such as Wikipedia (http://en.wikipedia.org/wiki/Scholarship) have a wealth of information, too."

Depending on your school's level of supportiveness in providing leads for scholarships and just how scholarship-rich your preferred college may be (usually not a problem), the scholarship search process can become quite time consuming, in which case, a supportive family—your parents, relatives, and siblings—can also prove advantageous in helping you to broaden and deepen your search for sources.

H I G H L I G H T

"At A Glance"

Scholarship leads can turn up in surprising places. One student discovered a scholarship contest announcement in a newsletter from her credit union that accompanied her monthly statement. Normally she discarded such advertisement-type literature, but this time she followed-up on the lead, obtained an application, applied, and won first place! Look everywhere for scholarship leads, and apply for every scholarship that comes your way, whether or not you think you have a chance!

If you already know your intended field of study or your college major, you can look for scholarships in this subject area through the corresponding department of the university you will attend. Also, talk with former students who have graduated from your high school or competed for scholarships in your field of interest. Talk with friends or older siblings who have "gone before." One set of parents with several successful "scholarshippers" in the family remarked, "It has been our experience that, one by one, as each youth in our family has competed for scholarships, each successive child has actually won more dollars and/or scholarships for college than the previous siblings because we have learned as a family to rely on and draw from the cumulative knowledge and experience that we have amassed from all of our children's previous scholarshipping efforts."

In another family's personal account, the oldest child was taught to think of herself as the "pathfinder" and to share her experience with the second oldest son, who in turn passed the additional knowledge that he gained to the next oldest daughter. All three of the "older children" then passed their knowledge on to their "youngest brother" who added his own personal experiences to his family's total pool of knowledge about scholarships. Incidentally, some of that collective knowledge and experience is now being passed on to *you*!

If you are fortunate to have the benefit of older brothers and/or sisters who competed successfully for scholarships, it is *imperative* that you *eliminate* any potential "sibling rivalry." Each of you should find great happiness in the other's success because it brings added honor (and financial relief) to the family as a *whole*. There is great wisdom in learning from another's mistakes without having to repeat them. By the same token, success should breed success!

Finally, be sure to utilize the power of Internet search engines to find thousands of scholarship opportunities and resources. Just typing in "scholarship" on any search engine can keep you busy for hours reading about free sources of scholarship information. Beware that many scams exist, so review potential scholarship sources and applications carefully.

REQUESTING SCHOLARSHIP APPLICATIONS

Unless you procure a scholarship application from your high school counselor, teacher, career center, or the Internet, you will generally need to request if for yourself. Hence, it is a good idea to develop a "form letter" or template that you can use over and over to request applications, whether on paper or via email. We have supplied a sample request letter with this book. However, be sure to tailor the letter to your "target audience" or organization.

Generally speaking, business correspondence letters, such as requests for a scholarship application, should be written in standard letter format, which includes:

1) A positive introductory greeting,

2) The request, and

3) A positive closing remark.

Make the letter concise, but in certain situations, it may be advantageous to include something about yourself so that the reader remembers your name when you finally submit your application. *Always avoid spelling errors!* And remember, your awards will be proportional to your consistency in requesting applications (as well as your persistence in applying for scholarships when the applications are received).

178 Scholar Drive
Collegebound, BA 93499-99876
12 January 2007

Marine Biology People Foundation
P.O. Box 54321
Generic, LN 12345-6789

Dear Sirs,

I understand that your organization is offering a scholarship to high school Seniors in the Greater Middle Region who wish to pursue studies in the natural sciences.

I will be entering Generica University in the Fall as a Marine Biology student and am extremely interested in applying for this award.

I would appreciate your sending a scholarship application to my home at the above address or to my email, scholarshipper@crandl.com. Thank you in advance for your kind consideration and reply!

Respectfully,
I.M. Scholarshipper

THOUGHT

PERSISTENT
    people begin their success
        where others end in failure.

—*Edward Eggleston*

All GreAt ThinGs are only a number of small things that have carefully been collected together.

Author Unknown

CONTENTS

THE SCHOLARSHIP APPLICATION

Typing, transcripts, letters of recommendation

No doubt you have heard of the time-honored cliché, *"A picture is worth a thousand words."* One single photograph of you can have a powerful effect upon perceivers. It can tell someone *exactly* what you would like him or her to know about yourself, whether you are conservative or liberal, self-confident or self-conscious, shy or friendly, athletic or studious. Each of these qualities might exist as part of you to some degree, but what you choose to emphasize usually becomes what others notice and remember. Your personal image undoubtedly carries a powerful and unique message about yourself. Scholarshipping is never about what you *intend* to convey, it is always about what is *perceived* by the institution to which you are applying.

The scholarship application follows the same concept of "a picture is worth a thousand words," only in the *reverse* sense. That is, you are now asked to provide the "thousand words" **first**, while the reader must build a mental "picture" of you in his or her own mind—an image that will hopefully convince the reader of your unique personal worth and merit. Although some scholarship committees may request one or more photos along with the application, most do not.

In addition to the standard information that you are asked to provide in your application, scholarship judges may also rely on recommendation letters and transcripts that accompany your application in order to become better acquainted with you and to assess your qualifications. Hence, your goal is to develop an entire application package that describes you with such accuracy and detail that the perceiver cannot help but think of you in terms of your potential for success, your caliber of achievement, and your current attitudes. This picture must be communicated so clearly and vividly that the judges not only understand you, but that they do not misunderstand you and/or your application.

This chapter addresses the three main components of most applications, namely:

I. The application itself,

II. The recommendation letter, and

III. The transcript.

Together, each part will provide you with the important secrets of producing a striking application packet that offers the reader a clear vision of who you are—which is, of course, A WINNER!

COMPONENT I: THE BASIC APPLICATION

Our experience is that the number one rule-of-thumb at this stage of the scholarship process is **neatness**. The neater you make your application, the better your image appears on paper. So:

Always type! Never use pen unless it is absolutely necessary or unless the instructions expressly direct you to print in pen and not type. "Most applications can either be completed online or downloaded and manually and fed through a printer. If completing an application online, be sure to eliminate any extra lines created when typing to maintain a polished look."

Keep the original clean! If possible, obtain or print an extra copy of the application to use as a worksheet. Then, complete that worksheet as a "trial run":

- ✐ Check your line spacing (single, double, triple) and align letters straight. If using a printer, word processor, or perhaps even an old typewriter, avoid the crooked, slanted line look at all costs.

- ✐ Adjust the point size as needed to fit the words and text into the allotted space requirements. Acceptable point sizes are usually 10 and 12 points.

✐ Experiment with different fonts for readability, but keep it simple and "clutter-free."

✐ Keep a consistent format and margins (for example, review your use of caps, mixed lettering, and/or italics).

If downloading or completing a hardcopy application, practice filling out one or more draft worksheets so you can get everything right on the final application. Practicing in this manner allows you to make mistakes while discovering what creates the best impression when you are finally ready for submission. Few documents seem as unattractive as an application covered with corrections, smears, grease stains, or sloppy marks. Sound like a lot of detail? You bet, but the time you take to meticulously check these details will definitely give you the competitive edge over the applicant who does not.

Fill out the application. This procedure should generally be the *easiest* part of the entire scholarship process because most applications usually ask some variation of the same information such as your name, social security number, school address, SAT/ACT score, GPA, and rank in class (see the next few pages for individual explanations). However, when vital information is not conveniently available when you need it, you can end up wasting valuable time searching for it. Looking high and low for that elusive piece of paper containing your latest SAT score, or that tiny scrap on which you've written the zip code of a recommendation letter source, can drive you crazy. Anyway, you get the picture!

Keep all information in one place. At the end of this chapter, we have supplied you with a *Personal Specification Sheet* to guide you through the basic data that you will need to have once you actually begin to complete your applications. Begin by compiling all of your essential information ***now*** in one place to save you future stress and frustration searching for it.

Here are a few helpful tips and explanations about commonly requested application components that are contained in your personal specification sheet:

> <u>YOUR NAME</u> Record your legal name. On an application, watch to ensure that you have correctly typed the ORDER of your name.

ADDRESS Be sure to indicate your mailing address if it is different from your residence.

SOCIAL SECURITY NUMBER (SSN) This space is made available to record your social security number, but due to increasing privacy concerns, it is always wise to keep your social security number secure. If you do not have a social security number, use the student ID number assigned to you by your school. In either case, for future reference, especially as you enter college and the work force, you should definitely acquire a social security number. You can apply for one at your local social security office, and you may need to take your birth certificate with you (see Chapter 2). Note: As mentioned earlier, some scholarship applications no longer use social security number due to privacy issues.

SCHOOL INFORMATION Beginning with the school that you are presently attending, write down information for ALL of your schools attended, including the addresses, phone numbers, principal's names, and month/year that you started and terminated your studies at each. For example, your present school may read: "from 09/06 to present," or if you transferred from a former school, the date should look something like "09/06 to 06/07", etc. You should also record the junior high schools and elementary schools that you attended—some scholarships ask.

GRADE POINT AVERAGE (G.P.A.) In the U.S. your GPA is a numeric expression of the letter grades that you have earned during the course of a semester or over your entire high school career. As a student, you will generally see two GPA's printed when your semester grades and transcripts are sent out: (1) Semester GPA, and (2) Cumulative GPA.

Your semester GPA is the average "point" for a particular semester only, so you will probably not need to know this for scholarship purposes.

What is more important is your "cumulative" GPA, the running score of ALL semesters that you have been a high school student (even if you have transferred schools).

Note that schools may have two additional GPA scores, one that includes any Advanced Placement (AP) course(s) that you have taken (you may receive an additional grade point for each AP course), and one that does NOT include your Freshman year grades. Inquire more about your school's grading policies from your guidance counselor.

On the specification sheet at the back of this chapter, space has been provided for you to write down your GPA and dates so that you can instantly recognize your latest score. If you are unable to find your score on your last report card or on a recent transcript, just ask your guidance counselor. You can also calculate your own GPA if necessary. Here's one formula for doing so:

CALCULATING YOUR GRADE POINT AVERAGE (GPA)

(Sample classes and grades are used below)

Your semester grades are:		GRADING SCALE:		POSSIBLE UNITS:
CALCULUS	A	A	4.0	0.0 - 3.0 (varies
FRENCH IV	B+	B	3.0	between schools)
HUMANITIES	A-	C	2.0	AP courses—
PHILOSOPHY	A	D	1.0	add one additional
PHYSICS	B-	CR	0.0	unit.
GOVERNMENT	C	("CR" edit courses		
ORCHESTRA	CR	are NOT factored into GPA)		

CALCULATION STEPS:

1. For each individual course, GRADING X UNIT = GRADE POINT

Example:

Calculus (A)	4.0 x 3.0 units= 12.0 grade points
French IV (B+)	3.0 x 3.0 units = 9.0 grade points
Humanities (A-)	4.0 x 3.0 units = 12.0 grade points
Philosophy (A)	4.0 x 3.0 units = 12.0 grade points
Physics (B-)	3.0 x 3.0 units = 9.0 grade points
Government (C)	2.0 x 3.0 units = 6.0 grade points
Orchestra (Cr)	0.0 x 2.0 units = 0.0 grade points

2. TOTAL UNITS & GRADE POINTS   20.0 units 60.0 grade points

3. TOTAL GRADE POINTS

$$\frac{\text{TOTAL GRADE POINTS}}{\text{TOTAL UNITS}} = \text{GPA} \qquad 60.0/20.0 = 3.0 \text{ GPA}$$

NOTE: To obtain CUMULATIVE GPA, continue calculating Step 1 for ALL classes before proceeding with Step 2 and 3.

Use this calculation method for a quick reference only or as a last resort. Your GPA is a critical piece of information that should be corroborated by a transcript.

RANK IN CLASS Based on your GPA, you are given a ranking against the total number of students in your class. If not indicated on a transcript or report card, your guidance counselor can supply you with your CURRENT RANKING as well as the TOTAL NUMBER OF STUDENTS in your class. To obtain a percentile, as some scholarships may ask, you should be able to follow this simple method:

RANK / TOTAL IN CLASS X 100 = %TILE

For example:

You rank 5th out of a Senior Class of 550
　　5 / 550 x 100 = .99 percentile
　　In other words, you rank in the
　　top 1% of your class.

You rank 23rd out of a Junior Class of 274
　　23 / 274 x 100 = 8.4 percentile
　　In other words, you rank in the
　　top 10% of your class.

TEST SCORE Report either your most recent or your highest standardized test score if you have retaken any of the tests (see Chapter 2).

HIGH SCHOOL CODE Your high school code is more often used for test application purposes and is infrequently asked on scholarship forms. However, it is definitely a handy number to have available. If you do not already know your high school code, ask your high school counselor or records office.

UNIVERSITIES APPLIED TO Record the name, address, and zip code of all colleges and universities to which you have applied as well as any institutions that may have already offered you admission.

EMPLOYMENT HISTORY In some cases, employment history is an important criterion and can reveal a great deal about your personal circumstances. Be sure that you provide all of the required information as accurately as possible.

HONORS/AWARDS/ACTIVITIES This section may become a significant portion of your total application, which is often treated as a separate addendum to the scholarship application form, itself. We have devoted an entire chapter to addressing the development of an effective "personal portfolio" (see Chapter 4).

Note: If you are an international student, you may not have some of this information readily available. For example, you may have to convert your high school's equivalent of a U.S. G.P.A. Regardless, do the best you can, and note any special circumstances in the scholarship application. Above all, be sure to keep your information in one place and readily accessible when you need it.

Submit your application as early as possible! Do not underestimate the significance of this principle. Simply stated, avoid procrastination! Procrastination is the deadliest of enemies to the would-be successful scholarshipper.

HIGHLIGHT

"A Day Too Late"

One year, a high school's top scholarship competitor applied for a national scholarship award. He was selected as one of several national finalists. However, when he was notified of this finalist status, he was requested to resubmit a second application AS SOON AS POSSIBLE. He was also informed that only a limited number of students who returned their applications first would receive monetary stipends. Yet, this student was so determined to create an immaculate second application that he worked on it until the very last day. Unfortunately, he did not receive a final award, and he maintains that his perfectionism (which delayed his responding) cost him the loss of a hefty monetary stipend.

Next year, this same individual's sibling also applied for the scholarship. She, too, was selected as a finalist. This time, she made certain that the final application was returned the very same day she received it. Subsequently, she became a scholarship winner. She attributed this positive outcome to her quick response time.

Some scholarships with multiple stages of competition require more than one application to be filed for each stage. For example, you might apply for a scholarship, become selected as a finalist, and then be required to submit yet another more detailed application in order to be eligible for selection as *the* final winner. In such cases, timeliness can become an especially important factor. Remember, applications are ultimately judged by *people*, and people tend to be impressed not just by appearances but also by quantity, quality, breadth, depth, and timeliness.

We have found that affording scholarship organizations the greatest possible time to evaluate your merits and qualifications always seems to work to your advantage.

Follow instructions. Because of the competitive nature of many scholarships, following instructions can become the critical control point in the qualification or ***dis***qualification of individuals from an applicant pool. In most cases, when filling out applications, more is better. But in some cases, instructions are quite explicit, and time tables are firmly established. When this occurs, give exactly what is required when it is required—no more, no less.

Adhere to guidelines religiously. For example, an application might ask you to complete your total hours of volunteer work for each entry that you provide or to briefly explain your responsibilities and roles in a separate column. Perhaps the instructions ask you to attach three letters of recommendation sealed in separate envelopes with a signature across the back flap. Or, you might be asked to return the application by certified mail *only*. In any case, remember to treat these instructions with strict attention. Many good applicants have either lost "points" or have even been completely eliminated from scholarship qualification processes due to a simple oversight of one small but important detail.

From our experience, many scholarship winners and judges have confirmed that adhering to instructions and details can be vital to the initial screening of applications. If an application possesses one glaring flaw, one significant breach of instructions, or one unfulfilled requirement, then mental or actual points can and are often deducted. Worse, the application might be eliminated altogether. Of course, this does not mean that you cannot be different or creative. Excel at being uniquely you, but be sure to do so within established application guidelines.

As we will discuss further, it is a good general practice to include as much information as you can so that judges have as many chances as possible to find something with which they can personally identify or relate. However, prudence and wisdom should always temper your urge to impress, especially when applications give explicit time tables or space constraints.

HIGHLIGHT

"The Beautiful Scholarship Form"

With his eyes set on winning the coveted prize few students in the state could ever hope to win, one high achiever felt certain that he was the top contender for a specific award because of his exceptional leadership.

He eagerly awaited the arrival of the application, and when it came, he poured all of his energies into making it as impressive as possible. He wrote so much that he required several additional pages of attachments. Unfortunately, he paid little attention to the small print on a section of the form which requested that no additional attachments be submitted and that all information be confined to the space allotted on the application.

Ignoring this instruction, the high-achiever submitted his "packet" anyway. His application never made it past the first level where further interviews and panel competitions would have ensued. Rather it was eventually returned unevaluated.

The following year, this fellow's sister was recommended by the school for the same state scholarship. This time around, she made a special effort to confine information to the space provided. Although her application was succinct, this young lady not only ended up qualifying as a finalist, but she proceeded all the way through the final interviews and a panel debate, emerging as the state winner!

Try to use the space provided before writing "see attached." Always fill in the blanks provided or mark "N/A" to show that a question has not been carelessly overlooked. Be cognizant of rules regarding space limitations or addendums. Should an application specifically ask that attachments be avoided, follow these instructions explicitly. On the other hand, if extra pages are allowed, take advantage of the opportunity to express yourself in detail.

Proof read. Ask a parent, friend, or even an English teacher to look for critical grammar errors or spelling mistakes in your application before producing your final copy for submission. Often, a second reviewer may catch anomalies that can save you from embarrassing and unnecessary point deductions.

Make a checklist of everything you need to do, collect, or send with your application. Some applications have a check-list that you can use. At other times, simply recording each step in writing can focus your attention on the essentials and help you to pace yourself.

Sign and date all appropriate forms. Believe it or not, many scholarshippers inadvertently overlook this small step. Signing and dating your application can make all the difference, especially when a scholarship organization has established strict deadlines, or when it regards timeliness as an important criterion (our experience is that many do!).

Copy the completed application packet. Always make a photocopy of any application you submit. Not only can reviewing copies refresh your memory, but the practice of retaining good historical documentation is a virtue in itself. This is an extremely important step to remember for your own record-keeping or personal history. Be sure to store all of your document copies in an organized fashion so that you can retrieve them quickly when and if they become needed.

COMPONENT II: LETTERS OF RECOMMENDATION

The vast majority of scholarships require that letters of recommendation be submitted with your application as a means of supplying valuable insights about yourself and personal testimonies about your character by those with whom you closely associate. These letters are written by individuals who can attest to your academic performance, work habits, personal accomplishments, individual personality, and unique talents.

WHOM DO I ASK?

Letters should generally be written by an individual who is a school teacher, community leader, and/or close associate who knows you well but who is not a relative of your family. As you become involved in school activities, in community service, and in the workplace, keep track of **activities** in which you participate as well as **people** you meet, because they will become part of the "pool" of individuals from which you may request letters of recommendation. Again, scholarships generally ask for three types of recommendation letters:

- ✐ SCHOOL RECOMMENDATIONS
- ✐ COMMUNITY RECOMMENDATIONS
- ✐ SPECIALIZED RECOMMENDATIONS

School Letters: Depending upon the nature of the scholarship, you may be asked to obtain recommendation letters from any of your teachers or administrators; that is, a principal, guidance counselor, teacher, club advisor, music director, coach, etc. Candidates may be drawn from persons who can objectively yet thoroughly evaluate and comment on your academic performance as well as leadership, citizenship, personal character, and achievements.

Community Letters: Community letters of recommendation are usually written by leaders with whom you have had significant interaction on either a long-term or short-term basis throughout the course of your community involvement. Such sources may include city council officials, other political or civic leaders, employers or work managers, local church leaders, scouting advisors, directors of volunteer organizations, symphony conductors, coaches, camp directors, 4H leaders, librarians, nurses, or anyone else *in the community* who knows you well and can recommend you without hesitation or reservation.

Specialized Letters: Because of the special nature of some scholarship programs, requesting letters of recommendation from individuals specifically aligned with or involved in a particular field could be a bonus strategy. For example, if you are applying for an athletic scholarship, letters written by your coach or trainer probably will probably carry more weight than letters from your private music teacher or math club advisor.

Inappropriate sources: Unless otherwise instructed, inappropriate sources of recommendation letters would include family members and relatives, student peers, someone who does not know you, and certainly someone who does not like you! Some scholarships request recommenders to seal their letters and return them directly to the requesting organization, so be sure that recommendations from your potential sources will be favorable to you, albeit truthful.

HOW TO REQUEST RECOMMENDATIONS

Since your recommendation letter sources may or may not be familiar with writing these types of letters, and since each scholarship letter may require different information content, you should be certain to supply your sources with as much information as possible about what you want to be done and how you would like your letter(s) constructed.

Requesting a recommendation letter is probably most effectively accomplished by obtaining a verbal commitment *and* by providing a written letter that contains all of the pertinent information that the source(s) should have. Include such material as:

1. Your full name

2. Your association with organization—employee, volunteer, student in class, etc.

3. Name of scholarship

4. To whom the letter should be addressed

5. Specific instructions about content (e.g. typed or hand written, on letterhead, less than one page, number of copies, etc.)

6. Your application or recommendation letter due date

7. A self-addressed stamped envelope OR address of the scholarship organization

8. Your telephone number for questions

9. An updated activity list for reference

Do not be surprised if some individuals ask you to write a few paragraphs about yourself to be included in the recommendation letter. In some instances, you may be asked to write the entire letter yourself, whereupon the recommender will edit and sign it. Remember that your recommender is probably a prominent person in your school or community, and as such, may have an extremely busy schedule and limited time.

The following sample letter on the next page incorporates the points listed above to illustrate a possible request for recommendation. Once you have sent your request letters, be sure to follow-up with a reminder phone call or letter as needed. Keep all available channels of communication open.

COMPONENT III: TRANSCRIPTS

Obtaining transcripts from your high school's records office is the third and perhaps simplest component of your application packet. However, be advised that you must usually order your transcripts weeks in advance to allow enough time for the transcripts to be processed. Rush requests may be costly, or worse, not honored by your school records office. **Plan ahead**, and purchase several transcripts at a time in anticipation of the many potential scholarships to which you will apply.

Unless otherwise specified, usually "official transcripts" are the only acceptable forms of transcripts that you may submit. "Official transcripts" must be an *original* print out of your grades, which bears the particular seal of your records office and/or signature of your records and admissions secretary. Official transcripts must usually be sealed in an official school envelope. Any other documents copied or contained in unofficial envelopes, such as quarterly report cards, will probably be unacceptable (again, this holds true unless stated differently by the awarding scholarship institution).

Remember that effective applications are created by attending to the details (not in broad "strokes" of activity). Of course, you should keep in mind your end objectives, but be sure to pay close attention to the details—the application form, your letters of recommendation, and your transcripts—in completing your scholarship applications.

88 Any Avenue
Notown, CA 90000
1 October 2007

Mr. John Doe, Supervisor of Volunteers
Valley Clinic Hospital
1234 Any Street
Notown, CA 90000

Dear Mr. Doe:

I am applying for the Famous Scholarship, an award recognizing distinguished academic and community achievement.

In order to fulfill competition requirements, a letter of recommendation from my community leader must accompany the application. I would greatly appreciate if you could take a few moments from your busy schedule to write a letter commenting on my personal character and my service as a candy striper during the past two summers at Valley Clinic Hospital.

The scholarship committee would like two copies of your letter sealed in separated envelopes with your signature in black ink across the sealed flap. Letters can be addressed to:

> Mr. I.M. Mac, Scholarship Coordinator
> CRANDL Publishers
> 123 ABC Street
> Anytown, NY 98765

In order to meet the deadline, please forward the letter to me before November 17, 2007.

I have enclosed a copy of my activity list as well as a self-addressed, stamped envelope for your convenience. If you have any questions, please feel free to contact me at (123) 456-7890 or scholarshipper@crandl.com. Thank you in advance for your kind consideration and assistance.

Sincerely,

I.M. Scholarshipper

encl: activity list

As mentioned earlier, keep track of all your scholarship application materials using the forms that follow. We have provided these worksheets to help you stay organized and ready for any type of data that may be requested on a scholarship application. If you find that some additional information is frequently requested that is not contained on these forms, feel free to add additional sheets as required—just be sure to track and keep all of the data in one place.

PERSONAL SPECIFICATION SHEET

Name_____Social Security Number ___ -_ _ - _____

Address_____Mailing Address_____

_____   _____

_____   _____

Phone (   )_____Message Phone (   )_____

HIGH SCHOOLS attended beginning with current school (Address, City, Zip Code):

1._____

_____

_____

Telephone:_____Principal:_____
High School Code:_____

2._____

_____

_____

Telephone:_____Principal:_____
High School Code:_____

3._____

_____

_____

Telephone:_____Principal:_____
High School Code:_____

4._____

_____

_____

Telephone:_____Principal:_____

High School Code:_____

GRADE AVERAGES:

Cumulative GPA:_____ as of_____semester

GPA with AP credits:_____ as of_____semester

Cumulative GPA:_____ as of_____semester

GPA with AP credits:_____ as of_____semester

Cumulative GPA:_____ as of_____semester

GPA with AP credits:_____ as of_____semester

Final Rank in Class:_____Total Students in Class:_____

Class Percentile:_____

TEST SCORES:

PSAT: (Date_____) Math_____Verbal_____Scaled Score:_____

(Date_____) Math_____Verbal_____Scaled Score:_____

SAT: (Date_____) Math_____Verbal_____

(Date_____) Math_____Verbal_____

(Date_____) Math_____Verbal_____

(Date_____) Math_____Verbal_____

ACT: (Date_____) Composite Score:_____

(Date_____) Composite Score:_____

(Date_____) Composite Score:_____

(Date_____) Composite Score:_____

COLLEGES AND UNIVERSITIES applied to:

1. Name:_____

Address:_____

_____

Telephone:(_____)_____Accepted: Y   N

2. Name:_____

   Address:_____

   _____

   Telephone:(_____)_____Accepted: Y   N

3. Name:_____

   Address:_____

   _____

   Telephone:(_____)_____Accepted: Y   N

4. Name:_____

   Address:_____

   _____

   Telephone:(_____)_____Accepted: Y   N

5. Name:_____

   Address:_____

   _____

   Telephone:(_____)_____Accepted: Y   N

1. Name:_____

   Address:_____

   _____

   Telephone:(_____)_____Accepted: Y   N

Hobbies:

   _____

   _____

   _____

Skills:

   _____

   _____

   _____

WORK EXPERIENCE:

Employer:_____From:_____ To:_____

Address:_____Phone:_____

   _____Supervisor:_____

Major responsibilities:_____

Employer:_____From:_____ To:_____

Address:_____Phone:_____

_____Supervisor:_____

Major responsibilities:_____

Employer:_____From:_____ To:_____

Address:_____Phone:_____

_____Supervisor:_____

Major responsibilities:_____

Employer:_____From:_____ To:_____

Address:_____Phone:_____

_____Supervisor:_____

Major responsibilities:_____

Employer:_____From:_____ To:_____

Address:_____Phone:_____

_____Supervisor:_____

Major responsibilities:_____

Employer:_____From:_____ To:_____

Address:_____Phone:_____

_____Supervisor:_____

Major responsibilities:_____

LETTERS OF RECOMMENDATION

Name of source/Title Letter(s) Sent To: Address/Phone	# of Copies	Request Date	Due Date
_____	_____	_____	_____	_____
_____				_____
_____				_____
(___)_____				_____
_____	_____	_____	_____	_____
_____				_____
_____				_____
(___)_____				_____

_____   _____ _____   _____
_____   _____
_____   _____
(___)_____   _____

_____   _____ _____   _____
_____   _____
_____   _____
(___)_____   _____

_____   _____ _____ _____   _____
_____   _____
_____   _____
(___)_____   _____

_____   _____ _____ _____   _____
_____   _____
_____   _____
(___)_____   _____

TRANSCRIPT REQUEST LOG:

Date Requested	Quantity Requested	Transcript(s) Sent To:
_____	_____	❑ _____ ❑ _____ ❑ _____ ❑ _____
_____	_____	❑ _____ ❑ _____ ❑ _____ ❑ _____
_____	_____	❑ _____ ❑ _____ ❑ _____ ❑ _____
_____	_____	❑ _____ ❑ _____ ❑ _____ ❑ _____
_____	_____	❑ _____ ❑ _____ ❑ _____ ❑ _____

SCHOLARSHIPS APPLIED TO:

Scholarship Name	Due Date	Award Granted		Monetary Amount
		Y	N	
_____	_____	❏	❏	$_____
_____	_____	❏	❏	$_____
_____	_____	❏	❏	$_____
_____	_____	❏	❏	$_____
_____	_____	❏	❏	$_____
_____	_____	❏	❏	$_____
_____	_____	❏	❏	$_____
_____	_____	❏	❏	$_____
_____	_____	❏	❏	$_____
_____	_____	❏	❏	$_____
_____	_____	❏	❏	$_____
_____	_____	❏	❏	$_____
_____	_____	❏	❏	$_____
_____	_____	❏	❏	$_____

DEVELOPING YOUR PERSONAL PORTFOLIO

4

WHATEVER YOU
vividly imagine,
ARDENTLY Desire,
SINCERELY believe, and
ENTHUSIASTICALLY act upon,

must inevitably come to pass!

Paul J. Meyer

CONTENTS

DEVELOPING YOUR PERSONAL PORTFOLIO

Honors, School and Community Involvement, Leadership

One day, a father went to pick up his daughter from work. They both came home upset because the father parked clear off to the side of the main entrance where he was all but invisible to his daughter who had no idea where he was parked (if he was even there). "All **you** had to do was **look** for **me**," declared the father when she finally found him. Simply put, he knew where *he* had parked, and he knew where his daughter would exit the building, but he had failed to make himself clearly visible to his daughter, since she was the one who needed to know!

This analogy parallels the relationship between your activity list and the scholarship process. No matter how much you accomplish as a student (even if you work twenty-four hours a day) you can *never* assume "that's all it takes" to convincingly sound like you are an active person. The secret to success rests in your ability to effectively communicate data about your activity in writing. If you fail to make yourself clearly visible by properly articulating all of your activities in an interesting fashion, you will be just like the parked car that nobody knew was there!

Remember that a scholarship activity list is *different* than a job resume. Whereas, you should generally limit job resumes to one or two pages at a maximum, scholarship activity lists can (and we believe should) be extended to as much or as long as possible. Why? Job resumes usually target a different audience than the scholarship activity list. Executives or business recruiters usually have tight schedules and demand terse, "business-like" correspondence. They are searching for individuals who can enter or work in a professional environment. On the other hand, organizations that offer scholarships (be they business enterprises, philanthropic societies, or civic groups) tend to have a different motive. They are mostly interested in developing and building youth.

To be sure, some groups or organizations offer scholarships purely for commercial gain or to appear philanthropic for public relations and advertising purposes. However, a plethora of easier ways to appear philanthropic also exist, and more often than not, an organization offers a scholarship out of a praiseworthy and genuine desire to advance the cause of youth and education. Of course, there may be specific goals or objectives in mind, but these institutions are genuinely interested in knowing all about you as a student and individual.

Hence, organizations that offer scholarships will probably prefer to view activity lists more closely than perhaps other information in the selection process. Always have a long and a short version of your activity list handy. The long version should not only include a list of activities and honors, but also a short explanation of your particular involvement or leadership role in each activity listed. What did it accomplish? What did you do? How was it done? What was unique about it? During high school, students generally submit an activity list with the long form (see attached examples). However, in college, some students also develop another innovative approach whereby they submit both a one-page pseudo job resume coupled with a longer, more comprehensive version of their activity list (yes, you can continue to apply for even more scholarships after you have matriculated into college).

Record every piece of data suggested at the end of this chapter in your portfolio, including the group/organization, leadership positions held, roles and responsibilities, significant contributions/activities, and the number of years of involvement.

BECOME INVOLVED IN EVERY- AND ANYTHING

Involve, recognize, and influence people to succeed! Engaging in a *variety* of activities and leadership develops well-rounded character. Well rounded individuals realize the value of balancing work, school, service and duty, as reflected in the quality and quantity of the kinds of contributions they make to their environment. A dancer who performs at hospitals, fairs and special events may be able to list a number of activities, but these kinds of contributions, in themselves, can be too easily regarded as "narrow" service. Flexibility and diversity of involvement shows a high demand for *you*. Remember that diversity of involvement affords you valuable working experience as well as plenty of leadership opportunities. By the way, if possible, try to track the overall hours of service that you render, as some scholarship application committees inquire.

When you serve, serve to the best of your ability so that community leaders remember you. You do not necessarily have to join an organization. Many groups would simply like you to call them and serve as a volunteer at special events or once a week for an hour or two. There is a difference between community or co-curricular "involvement" and community or co-curricular "service".

"Involvement" often means that you are related to a particular activity because of your personal membership in an organization such as the Amateur Golf Association, or a Youth Symphony. You have "joined" the organization per se. "Service," on the other hand, is not dependent on you being a bona fide member of a particular society, but rather, you are *volunteering* to help out whenever you are needed. For example, you may volunteer at the Special Olympics, or you may volunteer to help out for two hours a week at the local library even though you do not work there. This is service. If you can manage to find time to do both, then you have managed to make yourself into truly competitive material.

A scholarship panel's job is to determine which applicant is the most meritorious or deserving. Therefore, the more well rounded you seem—academically, socially, and in your contributions—the more you increase your chances of winning. In truth, the more service you can render to those around you, the more experience you will gain for yourself, regardless of the outcome of the scholarshipping process, and the more joy and happiness you will acquire throughout your life!

To demonstrate how easy it is to get involved, take a moment to browse through the following lists of organizations that may exist in your school or community and which could benefit from your involvement. These lists represent just the tip of the iceberg. Think of the thousands of other options that are specific to your region, community, interests or specialties. Explore them all!

THOUGHT

Don't worry about how
SUCCESSFUL
you are.

Just worry about how
USEFUL
you can be.

—Author Unknown

The ABC's of SCHOOL ACTIVITIES

A ASB Government, Academic Decathlon, Asian Student Union

B Band, Badminton team, Booster club

C Cheer leading squad, Choir, Chess club, Canned food drives, Computer club

D Debate team, Dance club, Desegregation Committee, Disabled Students Association

E Earth-Day Society, Energy Commission, Exchange student

F French club, Field sports, Fundraisers, Flag and Drill team, Forensics

G German club, Government offices for Fr./So./Jr./Sr., class, Gong Show

H Homecoming Committee, Honor Society, Hispanic Club

I International Relations club, Instrumental performer, Indian culture club

J Jazz ensemble, Journalism Association, Jr. class government

K Key Club, Karate team, Knowledge Bowl team

L Leisure activities club, Lab assistant, Literary club

M Model United Nations, Math contests, Mascot, Melodrama

N National Honor Society, Newspaper reporter

O Orchestra, Orientation services, Ombudsman

P Prom Committee, Parliamentarian, Photo club, Peer Counseling

Q Queen of Homecoming

R ROTC, Recycling Patrol, Rally organizer

S Sports/athletic teams, spirit club, Students Against Drunk Driving

T Theater productions, track events, tutor, tennis team

U Understudy for school play, university student (early admit or summer school)

V Varsity sports, Valentine's Day Dance Committee, Volleyball team captain

W Wrestling, Weight lifting, Water Conservation Corp

X Xylophone player in band/orchestra

Y Yearbook staff

Z Zoology club

The ABC's of COMMUNITY INVOLVEMENT

A American Heart Association, Adopt-A-Highway, American Cancer Society

B Blood Drives, Boy Scouts of America, Big Brothers and Big Sisters

C Community Centers, Crime Prevention Programs, Crisis Intervention, CPR Instructor

D   Dance Company, Day Care, Disable Persons Assistance Services, Drug Abuse Center

E   Explorer Scouts, Educational Associations, Ethnic Groups, Environmental Services

F   Future Farmers of America, 4-H Club, Food Drives, First Aid Instructor

G   Goodwill, Girl Scouts, Green Peace, Graffiti Removal Program, Golf Tournaments

H   Hospital volunteer, Homeless projects, Humane Societies, Ham Radio Club

I   Instructor of _____, Interest Group Associations, Ice-Skating Troupe

J   Jr. Achievement, Janitorial services, Judo team, Juvenile Diabetes Camp, Jr. League

K   Kid's camp counselor, Karate/Martial Arts Academy, Kidney Foundation

L   Library volunteer, Literacy Program, Lung Association, Language translator, Little League

M   Muscular Dystrophy Association, March of Dimes, Military, Minerals/Gems club, Museum

N   Nursing Homes, Non-profit organizations, Neighborhood Associations

O   Opera Company, Orchestra, (special) Olympics, Orphanage

P   Political organizations (campaigns), Pet services, Parks & Recreations, Piano Instructor

Q   Quilting Society

R   Religious Organizations, Red Cross, Rehabilitative Services, ROTC, Research Assistant

S   Sr. Citizen Services, Social Service Organizations, Soup Kitchens, Salvation Army

T   Telethons, Translator services, Tennis club, Theater

U   Upward Bound Tutor, United Way, UNICEF

V   Veterans and Military Organizations, volunteer exchange, voter registration drives

W Welfare Organizations, Walk-A-Thon, Wildlife Protection Agency

X Xylophone player in community orchestra

Y YMCA, Youth Commission, Young Astronauts, Young life

Z Zoo volunteer

GO FOR LEADERSHIP EXPERIENCE

A strong applicant is more often than not one who has held some type of leadership responsibility and who remembers to identify on the activity list his or her role in the organization by title. As discussed in chapter 2, many levels of leadership exist as well as styles of exhibiting leadership skills both formally and informally. However, in the scholarshipping arena, titles can and do help. Here are some proper titles often used when creating personal portfolios:

President, Vice President, Treasurer, Secretary, Historian, Fundraiser, Deputy President (VP), Vice President of Finance, Social Secretary, Events Coordinator, Student Representative, Justice of the Peace, Parliamentarian, Presenter, Publicity Chairperson, Liaison, Advisor, Committee Member, Instructor, Delegate at Large, Associate Member, Affiliate, Patron, Board Member, Executive Committee Member, Student Assistant, Researcher, Recipient, Supervisor, Manager, Captain, Lieutenant (military titles), Concertmaster, Member, Volunteer, Participant, Chairperson, Editor, Publisher, Team Member, Founder, Eagle Scout, Lead Performer, Tutor, Youth Commissioner, Consultant, Trainer, etc.

USE ACTION VERBS

Whenever possible, use active verbs versus passive verbs in describing your activities and/or involvement. Not only do they sound grammatically appealing, but they also represent you as a mover and a doer, someone who knows where he or she is going and what he or she wants to accomplish.

LESS EFFECTIVE	MORE EFFECTIVE
Emergency Preparedness Fair First Aid Booth	*Planned, organized*, and *implemented* First Aid Exhibit for community wide Emergency Preparedness Fair

Still having trouble finding the right words? Just try to verbally explain it to Mom and Dad or your sibling(s), and somewhere along the way, you are bound to find the perfect verb. Try some of these action verbs, too:

PASSIVE VERBS (limit use):	**ACTION VERBS** (use frequently):
to participate in, hope, have, know, understand, realize, be, and/or any other verb that seems vague or undescriptive....	to plan, write, publish, assist, implement, coordinate, solve, instigate, organize, represent, manage, make, supervise, sponsor, preside over, create, conduct, develop, advise, attain, attend, explain, judge, prevent, provide, pioneer, cook,establish, operate, practice, prepare, produce, recognize, select, and so on!!

SHOULD I INCLUDE TRIVIALITIES?

This point of consideration is perhaps one of the most frequently asked questions regarding activity lists and one of the trickiest to answer. In the end, YOU must be the final judge of what to include or not to include in your activity list. However, we have generally found that it is better to include too much than not enough.

Simply stated, "Let the judge be the judge." Just be certain to present ALL of the pertinent facts. Your parents and family members may be very helpful in reminding you of past activities which you perhaps thought were insignificant, but which were actually significant in defining your character, capabilities, and/or personality. What one individual esteems as naught, another may prize as having great value and worth.

Aside from recommendation letters (which may be grossly biased), many scholarship reviewers only have the application and activity lists with which to make large inferences or conclusions about the whole person—YOU. So, you must make your best attempt to reflect your true character through your activity list.

T I P

Little things in an activity list can and do make a big difference, depending upon the type of scholarship. From a judge's point of view, when reading piles of applications, many of the activities and awards can become redundant. But when judges read about something that an applicant has done that is unique or original (however insignificant it may seem to you at the time), this may give the activity a little more consideration and weight in the minds of judges.

SPELL CHECK EVERYTHING

In just a few years, computers have permeated almost every household and have become a must-have commodity. If you own or have access to a word processor or a computer, *use it*. If you do not, try to get access to one. If you can't, all is not lost (but start early!). Make everything as neat and as clean as possible. Hire a typist if you must. It will be well worth the expense. Try, if possible, to have your activity list printed on a laser printer, but remember appearance alone without substance rarely wins a scholarship. Our experience is that appearances will help the most if the quality or caliber between the activity lists of two or more different contestants seems fairly close. Of course, NEVER misrepresent yourself, but ALWAYS present yourself in the best possible light.

AVOID ACRONYMS

Spell it out! Official names of organizations should be used instead of acronyms, unless the acronym is a nationally known term. For example, UNICEF and USA are words that are both nationally and internationally known, but acronyms like CSF or ADA may not be generally recognized. CSF is well-known in California, but perhaps not as well known in other states; ADA—does it mean American Diabetic Association, American Dietetic Association, or American Dental Association? If you were a judge reviewing scholarship applications, which one of the following entries on an applicant's activity list would impress you more?

<u>A</u>	<u>B</u>
E.S.C. Social Secretary	Social Secretary, Engergy Saving Commission—organized annual campus-wide energy conservation day which saved the school over $1000.

Of course, the "B" seems more impressive. Why? Response "A" gives the reader no clue as to what ESC means. Moreover, the entry suggests that this person had nothing more than titular involvement in the organization. This is a parked car! The reader cannot plainly tell much about this person's contribution, and after looking at possibly hundreds of applications, scholarship judges are usually not in the mood to play guessing games.

Response "B" creates a clearer picture of the applicant's contributions simply because it is spelled out *in detail*. It is easy to see how this individual's leadership made a difference. Let's try another one:

<u>A</u>	<u>B</u>
French Club Member	French Club Member—attended meetings, helped fundraise

In this case, either entry might be appropriate because, if you are unable to specify a SIGNIFICANT or noteworthy contribution outside of "regular" duties and responsibilities (for example, took notes or attended meetings), it is really not advantageous to write down the details. Save the space for more important data.

A significant note might be:

French Club member—100% attendance at meetings; received the Outstanding Freshman Fund-raiser Award for raising over 50% of the club's annual funds.

This statement says that you were not only a good club member but also an *enthusiastic* member who went above and beyond the call of duty.

BE CONCISE

Sometimes the most powerful statements are the most simple as well. Less can be more. Don't go overboard with adjectives that either glorify something or attempt to make your activities look better, sound bigger, or seem more impressive.

COMMON TERMINOLOGY

Similar to acronyms, words related to a particular organization or institution are not always readily understood by the general public and may be considered jargon. For example, President of the Order of the Arrow should be clarified with another phrase to explain what it is: an Honor Camper and service organization sponsored by the Boy Scouts of America. If you have to ask yourself "Do you think they will understand what that is?" chances are you will need to elucidate your meaning with different terminology.

When one student was composing his lists, he would meticulously refine each entry until his contributions, activities, and honors were as clear as crystal. He even wrote, "Eagle Scout—the highest rank attained in Scouting", so that if by chance the judge was someone who was not familiar with what this kind of award meant, he or she would not be left to interpret its significance as something meritorious or not.

EXPLAIN AND EXPOUND ON DUTIES/ACTIVITIES

Numbers and quantities are always preferred in an activity list, and of course, the larger the number, the better the effect. Use numbers whenever possible and practical, but do not over exaggerate or use figures to express trivialities. List the most important items first and then the least significant ones last.

AVOID REPEATING ENTRIES

List specific entries only once, and put the number of years involved next to each entry in parentheses. Some scholarships require you to provide chronological activity lists, in which case you might need to repeat entries under different years. Try to group like activities together.

SOME SUGGESTED FORMATS

The following are three common ways of structuring an activity list:

1) Position, Organization—explanation...
      ...explanation continued (indented)

2) Organization
      Position—explanation, year involved

      Position—explanation, year involved

3) Org/Position (years of participation)

Use the **Activity List Worksheets** provided for you at the end of the chapter to record *in detail* every award or honor received, school or community activity accomplished, and leadership position held. To help you visualize what an activity list might look like, we have included an actual activity list patterned after format #2 (years not included). Remember, this is only ONE of many unique formats possible. It is your task to tailor the suggested patterns in ways that present you in the most visible "parking space".

MAINTAIN A UNIFORM FORMAT

Be consistent. Use the same format, tenses, fonts, font sizes, margins, and line spacing throughout. Some applications—for example, an application for a graphic design scholarship—may require more creativity in formatting, but in general, keep your applications uniform.

PHOTOCOPIES

Make numerous extra copies of your activity lists so that you will always have them available and on hand to send or provide to individuals and associates from whom you have requested (or will request) written letters of recommendation.

CONSTANTLY UPDATE YOUR ACTIVITY LIST

Once you have created your initial list, do not allow it to remain static or become passé. Regularly revise it and update the list, adding your most current leadership awards, honors, activities, and positions. There will always be additional occasions to use your list for jobs, college, school, or historical reference. Your activity list is a valuable record and a testament to all of the effort you have committed to the activities in which you have been involved. Many scholarship winners have referred to their activity lists years later in helping their own children prepare for scholarships!

COVER LETTER

If a cover letter is warranted, make every attempt to avoid negatives or flag words in the cover letter and in your activity list. Leave negativism alone. Stay positive, concise, and upbeat. Use optimistic words whenever possible. If a negative situation must be addressed in order to illustrate a particular point, try to avoid the words "NO, NOT, DIDN'T, DON'T, CAN'T," etc. by perhaps using softer words like "AVOID, UNABLE," etc. Employing the right words can convey power and impact quickly in an activity list or cover letter.

There is no one right way to construct a cover letter, but be sure to follow the same rules stipulated for recommendation letters: avoid spelling mistakes, keep them brief, be assertive but courteous, cater your letters to the scholarship situation at hand, and address your letters to the right individuals as appropriate. If you are unsure whether a cover letter is necessary, create one just in case.

The forms that follow are provided to help you capture your activities and to keep them organized according to the tips and techniques provided in this chapter. Of course, our method is only one of many ways to record your activities, particularly in light of the modern database technologies available today. Be creative, but do track your activities, and be sure that they are readily accessible when you need them the most. Remember, in the scholarshipping arena, both the *quantity* and *quality* of your applications counts. These forms will help you to achieve both.

ACTIVITY LIST

Begin to record your activities using the format below. Add to or review it on a regular basis. Use additional paper as necessary.

Honors and Awards

Award Name	Organization	Date (M/D/Y)	Description
_____	_____	_____	_____
_____	_____	_____	_____
_____	_____	_____	_____
_____	_____	_____	_____
_____	_____	_____	_____
_____	_____	_____	_____
_____	_____	_____	_____
_____	_____	_____	_____
_____	_____	_____	_____
_____	_____	_____	_____
_____	_____	_____	_____

School

Club or activity	Title/position	Dates of participation	Responsibilities/ projects
_____	_____	_____	_____
_____	_____	_____	_____
_____	_____	_____	_____
_____	_____	_____	_____
_____	_____	_____	_____
_____	_____	_____	_____
_____	_____	_____	_____
_____	_____	_____	_____
_____	_____	_____	_____
_____	_____	_____	_____
_____	_____	_____	_____
_____	_____	_____	_____
_____	_____	_____	_____
_____	_____	_____	_____
_____	_____	_____	_____
_____	_____	_____	_____
_____	_____	_____	_____
_____	_____	_____	_____
_____	_____	_____	_____
_____	_____	_____	_____
_____	_____	_____	_____
_____	_____	_____	_____
_____	_____	_____	_____
_____	_____	_____	_____
_____	_____	_____	_____
_____	_____	_____	_____

Community

Club or activity	Title/position	Dates of participation	Responsibilities/ projects
————————	————————	————————	————————————
————————	————————	————————	————————————
————————	————————	————————	————————————
————————	————————	————————	————————————
————————	————————	————————	————————————
————————	————————	————————	————————————
————————	————————	————————	————————————
————————	————————	————————	————————————
————————	————————	————————	————————————
————————	————————	————————	————————————
————————	————————	————————	————————————
————————	————————	————————	————————————
————————	————————	————————	————————————
————————	————————	————————	————————————
————————	————————	————————	————————————
————————	————————	————————	————————————
————————	————————	————————	————————————
————————	————————	————————	————————————
————————	————————	————————	————————————
————————	————————	————————	————————————
————————	————————	————————	————————————
————————	————————	————————	————————————
————————	————————	————————	————————————
————————	————————	————————	————————————
————————	————————	————————	————————————
————————	————————	————————	————————————

SAMPLE ACTIVITY LIST ONLY

HONORS AND AWARDS

IBM Thomas J. Watson Scholar

Eagle Scout with Bronze, Gold and Silver Palms

Electronics Representatives Association Scholar

[NAME] University Honor Music Conservatory Award

[NAME] University Presidential Scholar

[NAME] Sr. Memorial Award for Outstanding Community Service, from [NAME] Inc.

Rotary International Speech Contest: District 1st Place, Regional 1st Place, Final Competition 2nd Place

Elks Most Valuable Student Award: Local, District, & State 1st Place; National Finalist Winner

Bank of America Fine Arts Award: Plaque Winner; Zone Contest 1st Place; Final Competition 2nd Place

County Science and Engineering Fair: 1st Place Award from [COMPANY NAME] & [NAME] Electronics Company; 1st Place Award from the American Institute of Mining, Metallurgical and Petroleum Engineers; Outstanding Award from US Marine Corps; Silver Medallion from US Air Force; Honorable Mention from Fair Association

Command Performance Award, highest honor/rating possible from State Music Educators Association

Educational Communications Foundation Scholarship Finalist

Finalist, Jostens Foundation Scholarship Competition

Century III Leaders Award, National Association of Secondary School Principals

Daughters of the American Revolution Good Citizens Award

Asian American Club Scholarship

Honor Color Guard for City Mayor's Inauguration

County Youth Hall of Fame member & Awards Ceremony Keynote Speaker

County Youth Hall of Fame Scholarship Judge

Grand Champion, State Talent Competition

Local [NAME] TV Channel Volunteer Service Award

Order of the Arrow Service Award

County Fair Association Service Award

United States National Achievement Academy Scholar

United States National Leadership Award

United States National Leadership and Service Award

National Secondary Education Councils Academic All-American Award

County Board of Education Academic Excellence Award

Presidential Academic Fitness Award

United States National Mathematics Award

Honors 2nd Award—Fine Arts, County Academic Decathlon

Society of Distinguished American High School Students Award

Certificate of Merit, [NAME] Valley Youth Exposition Poetry Competition

High School District Board of Trustees: Distinguished Academic Achievement Award; Distinguished Community Service Award; Distinguished Fine Arts Achievement Award

Youth in Concert Outstanding Musicians Award

Boy Scouts of America Duty to God Award, Trail Award, On My Honor Award, and World Conservation Award

Who's Who Among American High School Students Scholar

High School Award for Activities and Service

High School District Superintendent's Honor Roll, 4 years

High School Associated Student Body Council Service Award

2nd Place District Level Math Field Day Competition

Magna Cum Laude Scholar

Voted Most Likely to Succeed in High School Senior Class

Seminary/Religious Studies Graduation Awards

2nd Place overall, Regional Explorer 50 Mile Canoe Race

> ### SAMPLE ACTIVITY LIST ONLY

> ## COMMUNITY ACTIVITIES

Church/Religious:

Young Men's Organization—Quorum President, 1st Counselor, Secretary, Young Men's Committee member

Bishops Youth Council member

Selected to compete in Regional Dance Festival

Tenor in Church choir

Provide spiritual & temporal assistance to families

Deacon, Teacher, Priest, Elder

Boy Scouts of America:

National Eagle Scout Association

    Secretary, Council Executive Board;

    Organized Annual Eagle Scout Association Banquet at [PLACE];

    Eagle Scout Seminar Trainer

World Boy Scout Jamboree in Calgary, Canada

    Junior Staff representing US, Council Contingent Secretary;

    Designed over 2000 friendship tokens and the delegation logo;

    Designed and constructed delegation's welcoming gateway

National Explorer President's Association, Council Secretary Order of the Arrow National Honors Campers Organization

    Council Lodge Secretary/Treasurer;

    Editor of a publication for over 400 members;

    Area Camping Promotions Chair/Section Representative;

    Scout-O-Rama Chair, organized information booth & camping exhibit

Helped establish [NAME] Medical Explorer Post

Alternate Staff Member, Council Summer Camp

BSA Staff-in-Training program member

Council Junior Leadership Training program member

Council Extravaganza staff member

National BSA Training at Philmont, New Mexico—graduate

Designed & directed landscaping of BSA garden display for competition

County Council Memorabilia Auction, at [NAME] State Hospital

Scout Recruitment Chairman, District Camporee Staff

Explorer Paramedical Post, member

President, Explorer Post [NUMBER] and Venture Troop [NUMBER]

Troop [NUMBER] Senior Patrol Leader, Instructor, Leadership Corps

Assisted in numerous Eagle Projects

    Redeveloped [NAME] Park nature trail—added flora/fauna display;

    CPR certification courses and Blood drives;

    Constructed and installed Trophy Case in local school library

Civic Organizations

County Youth Ambassador

County Special Olympics volunteer

Red Cross, organized & instructed CPR certification courses; have certified over 200 people—some have used the skill. Also blood drive sealer.

Jack Emergy Canned Foods Drive for Underprivileged Children

City Preparedness Fair, organized disaster awareness exhibit

City Council Youth Commissioner by Mayoral Appointment

    First Vice Chairman;

    Performed in quartet at and organized City Premiere of [NAME], a benefit fund raiser to construct a city youth center, grossed over $[AMOUNT];

    Youth-in-Government Day, Youth Commission Representative;

    Youth Recognition Scholarship Sponsor, Co-master of Ceremonies with [NAME] of TV Station [NAME] at annual awards ceremony;

    Helped legislate numerous city-wide youth issues

County Fair Association—2nd largest fair in [STATE]

    Active Association member & Horticulture volunteer

    Public relations/Marketing volunteer journalist, media liaison; compiled daily newsletter for entire fair

American Lung Association, implemented lung/respiratory, optical, blood pressure testing at Senior Health Fair

City Museum volunteer for ground breaking ceremony and Kid's Day Festival

Community Library, participated in ground-breaking ceremony & Friends of the Library volunteer (book sales)

City Parks & Recreation, organized South Side Community Center Halloween Haunted House

[NAME] Hospital & County Mass Casualty Committee, simulated community emergency drill to test public disaster preparedness

Fine Arts

City Youth Symphony, Associate Concertmaster 2 years and performed with orchestra 6 years

> International Music Festival, Vienna, Austria—invited to compete, [YEAR] Toured Hollywood in Concert, performed with Hollywood Youth Symphony

> Performed for [NAME] Lodge Association

[NAME] Hill Chamber Ensemble, Concertmaster

Region Messiah Oratorio, Concertmaster 3 years

[NAME] Pageant Orchestra, Concertmaster

West [NAME] Symphony, guest soloist 3 times

City of [NAME] Founders Day Celebration, guest performer

County Board of Education, organized & performed in quartet for TV Station video taping

[NAME] Symphony Orchestra, Concertmaster, 5 years

> Designed & landscaped outdoor garden exhibit; won 2nd place in competition

> Represented Orchestra in radio interviews & TV show

> Lions Club Executive meeting, performed on behalf of Orchestra

> International Music Festival, Vienna, Austria—invited to compete, [Year]

State Youth Symphony, violinist

Community Christmas Cantata, Concertmaster

Children's Cancer Society, performed in "King and I" & "Camelot" benefit productions

Senior Citizen Home, guest performer

"Oklahoma" Community-wide production for over 1200 people, Concertmaster

State Orchestra Directors Association Honor Orchestra, Concertmaster

[NAME] String Quartet, founder and 1st violin

Invited to play with South Valley & [NAME] University Symphonies

City Opera Theater, Concertmaster for "Amahl & the Night Visitors"

City Conservatory for Performing Arts member

[NAME] Theater Repertoire Orchestra, violinist

Saint Seans Oratorio Community Concert, principle 2nd violin

Several Recital Chamber orchestras, violinist

International Amateur Chamber Music Players Association, member

Private Violin Teacher

SAMPLE ACTIVITY LIST ONLY

SCHOOL INVOLVEMENT

High School

Varsity Wrestler

Concertmaster—all school musicals

Student Appreciation Concert—annual guest soloist

Stock market Competition Team Captain—Transaction Committee Chairman

County Academic Decathlon—School Team Captain & Honors Division Rep

Parent/Student Advisory Committee—Principal's Student Representative

Associated Student Body Council (ASB)

> Vice President—organized school-wide car wash reaching a record of over 1500 cars washed

> Senate Chairman, organized Freshman Guides program

> Assistant President

> Freshman Class President

> Supreme Court Justice & ASB Parliamentarian

> Homecoming , Dance, and Rally Committee

Unpaid tutor in Math, Computers and English

Organized and instructed week-long CPR course for 5 Anatomy and Physiology classes; donated class set of 30 textbooks and created tests and lesson plans for the science department to use in future years.

National Honor Society

> Vice President

> Induction Ceremony Program Committee Chairman

> Scholarship fund-raising committee

State Scholarship Federation

> President & Life member

> Scholarship Committee—applicant screening judge

> Scholarship Fund Raising Committee-organized school-wide plant and candy sales drive

French Club

> President—organized Culture exhibit for school display, Christmas socials, Mardi-Gras, inter-club sports tournament

> Fundraising committee member

Math Club

    Scholarship Committee—applicant screen judge

    Helped organize Christmas social, bake sales, & flea market

    District Math Field Day Competition—school Trigonometry Team member

    Polytechnic University Math Competition

Computer Club, instructor of a Teacher's Graphic Programming course

International Relations/Model United Nations

    Delegate to Conference representing US

    Fundraising committee member

School Energy Commission

    Secretary

    Represented school at District Energy Convention

Mathematics, Engineering, and Science Association, associate member

THE ESSAY

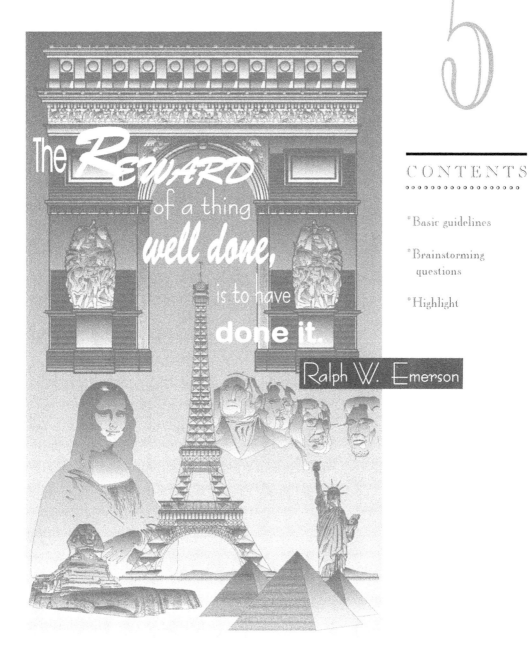

The REWARD of a thing well done, is to have done it.

Ralph W. Emerson

5

CONTENTS

THE ESSAY

How to answer questions

The purpose of writing an essay is to let the reader sample or make an assessment of your command of English, your logic, your opinions, and just plain *you*. Never assume that the reader is interested in your answer only, but rather, *how* you express your ideas as well. Are you grammatically correct? Are your sentences complete and well-developed? Are you creative, logical, thoughtful, and insightful? Distracting language can reduce your credibility tremendously. Not all applications require an essay, but when they do, be sure to express yourself so that your essay *sings*.

In one highly coveted scholarship program, applicants were asked to describe their contributions to their family life. Nine out of every ten applicants responded in the same ambiguous way: "I often babysit my siblings," "I contribute financially by working after school," or "I try to be supportive to my family." The judges remained unimpressed, and needless to say, these applicants received an "average" score for their "average responses." Since essays are opportunities to reflect your most creative thinking, they can often mirror your personality and attributes in ways that a scholarship application or grades may not. However, essays can consume a tremendous amount of time in the application process.

Without sensationalizing, try to be original and specific. Incidentally, the winner of the scholarship in the "highlight" box below did not receive the highest score for her essay. So, it is technically possible to be average in one area and still win scholarships. However, the point is that thoughtfulness and creativity always seems to pay-off in the essay writing arena.

HIGHLIGHT

"Impressions in Writing"

During an interview, one student was actually complimented by her interviewer who said, "I really enjoyed reading your application because your response reflected considerable thought and effort on your part. I've read so many applications that don't really say anything. Yours was refreshing." Simply stated, her application stood out among all the other applicants because she took the time to provide unique and earnest responses to simple questions. She was not a brilliant writer, but she was sincere, creative, and grammatically correct in her approach.

AVOID RE-INVENTING THE WHEEL

Like writing any composition, it is always desirable to first *brainstorm* for ideas, write a rough draft, and then let it incubate for a short time before actually writing your essay. However, unless the original question relates specifically to one issue or another, or unless it is completely new to you, you might want to consider trying to re-work previous essays that you have written about yourself and to make them fit into the space(s) provided. Be sure to follow instructions and meet all of the required criteria for each essay. This method not only saves you valuable time but also allows you to make small improvements and refinements every time you utilize a particular essay.

On the other hand, if you were not completely satisfied with the way an essay turned out on your last application, or if you suspect that an essay evoked particularly negative reactions from the judge(s) of your last scholarship competition, it might be wise to construct another composition that works more to your advantage. Stay open and be willing to change your writing style or approach as needed.

WRITE CLEARLY AND INTELLIGENTLY

At this stage of your life, your writing style should reflect something higher than the subject-verb, subject-verb sentence structure. Try beginning your sentences with a gerund phrase or a prepositional clause. Do not be afraid to reopen your grammar book to review grammar tips. Many otherwise promising scholarship essays often lack proper development and flow.

CHECK FOR GRAMMAR AND SPELLING

Remember to proof read and/or rewrite your essays as often as necessary to ensure that all spelling errors or grammatical inconsistencies are eliminated. Hemmingway rewrote his manuscripts literally hundreds of times before publication. Reading aloud helps. Parents or siblings can offer valuable perspectives on content, essay structure, and grammatical correctness. Allow for sufficient time between each review of your draft or proof-reading for your mind to clear and your eyes to rest so that each review comes from a fresh perspective. This practice can also prevent you from becoming so attached to particular concepts, expressions, or sections of your essays that you become inflexible to any changes or edits that may ultimately improve them.

NEVER PLAGIARIZE!

Always give proper credit where credit is due. When you borrow a quote or concept, cite the originator if known.

AVOID COMMON LANGUAGE

Slang has no place in formal essays. What type of person would you envision if you read the following essay on the subject of achievement: "I think achievement is really great and totally awesome. . . ."

LET YOUR CREATIVE JUICES FLOW

Some students have found that the best time to receive inspiration in writing essays is early in the morning when their minds are rested and their bodies are refreshed. Whatever seems to be the most conducive time for letting your creative juices flow, however, be sure to avoid the last minute rush and late night cramming. This precarious habit may altogether destroy a potentially good application or otherwise promising essay.

Fiddle around, but make haste. Create lists, doodle, and write ideas on index cards. Talk with other people from various walks of life and with different perspectives. Seek their advice. Reflect upon these "inputs" as well as your own life experiences, but remember, move decisively and AVOID PROCRASTINATION!

PRACTICE BRAINSTORMING

Here are a few generic essay questions to get you thinking about possible topics for scholarships. Use additional paper as necessary, and try thinking of other possible scholarship essay questions:

✍ Summarize your educational experience and relate it to your future goals:

_____

_____

_____

_____

_____

_____

_____

_____

_____

_____

_____

_____

_____

_____

_____

_____

🖎 What is your chosen field of study? Recount an experience that influenced your decision:

_____

_____

_____

_____

_____

_____

_____

_____

_____

_____

_____

_____

_____

_____

_____

🖎 What would you consider your most important contribution to your school or community?

_____

_____

_____

_____

_____

_____

_____

_____

_____

_____

_____

_____

_____

_____

_____

_____

_____

✐ Describe three personal characteristics that make you successful.

_____
_____
_____
_____
_____
_____
_____
_____
_____
_____
_____
_____
_____
_____
_____
_____
_____
_____

✐ What do you consider to be your most important contributions to your family?

_____
_____
_____
_____
_____
_____
_____
_____
_____
_____
_____
_____
_____
_____
_____
_____
_____
_____
_____

✐ Why should you be chosen above all other candidates for this scholarship?

_____
_____
_____
_____
_____
_____
_____
_____
_____
_____
_____
_____
_____
_____
_____
_____
_____
_____
_____

✐ How can this scholarship contribute to your personal and/or professional aspirations?

_____
_____
_____
_____
_____
_____
_____
_____
_____
_____
_____
_____
_____
_____
_____
_____
_____
_____
_____

✐ What do you consider to be the three most significant accomplishments in your life and why?

_____
_____
_____
_____
_____
_____
_____
_____
_____
_____
_____
_____
_____
_____
_____
_____
_____
_____
_____

✐ Describe one of your role models and how you were influenced by this individual.

_____
_____
_____
_____
_____
_____
_____
_____
_____
_____
_____
_____
_____
_____
_____
_____
_____
_____
_____
_____

EFFECTIVE INTERVIEWING

6

The **A**RT OF **C**ONVERSATION
consists as much of
listening politely
as in
TALKING AGREEABLY.

George Atwell

CONTENTS

° Interviewing formats

° First impressions

° Practice questions
° Personal review
and progress page

EFFECTIVE INTERVIEWING

Preparation, Presentation skills, Questions

One scholarshipper believes that the best way to prepare for interviewing is to do it often! Our objective in this chapter is to share skills with you on how to be effective and successful during an interview and to provide you with a variety of exercises and activities to help fine tune your interviewing abilities. Remember, the more you practice, the more equipped you become with these simple, yet powerful, tools.

LEARN INTERVIEWING FORMATS

Many interviews are conducted using one of two basic formats:

1) The Personal format, in which candidates are interviewed on an individual basis by judges, or

2) The Group format, in which candidates are interviewed together and asked to discuss a given topic.

In other cases it is possible to learn about the interviewing format ahead of time and thereby prepare mentally for the experience.

FAMILIARIZE YOURSELF WITH THE THREE BASIC TYPES OF QUESTIONS

It would be silly to ask you to memorize a list of a million questions that interviewers could possibly ask during an interview and expect you to recite each answer by heart. Therefore, in order to eliminate the need for this monumental ritual, the most common types of questions asked have been classified here into three general categories:

I.   PERSONAL QUESTIONS

II. HYPOTHETICAL QUESTIONS

III. DISCUSSION/INFORMATIVE QUESTIONS

Depending on the interview format and style (individual or group), you may be asked any combination of these question types.

I. PERSONAL questions are perhaps the most common types of question posed in both the group and individual formats. They involve simple, yet important, inquiries into your personal history and character. For example, you may be asked to share your educational plans and future career goals, or to relate a past experience that has influenced you, or to describe a personal strength or weakness.

Regardless of the specific question, bear in mind times that moments like these are meant for you to *sell yourself*. Let's face it. No judge (at least we hope not) is ever going to directly ask you if you are a great leader or a responsible person. *You* must be the one to verbalize just how good a leader or how responsible a personal you are by the manner in which you answer the question(s).

II. Common to both individual and group settings is the category of **HYPOTHETICAL** questions, a more subtle method of inquiry employed to find out about you as well as your thought processes. Hypothetical questions are easily identified by certain "cue" phrases (for example, **"If** you had___,what would you do?" or **"Suppose** you were.........?") and then require that you supply an ending thought or a resulting consequence. Your response becomes an ensuing action based upon your unique background and set of core beliefs. As these questions tend to be more surrealistic than realistic, you will need to exhibit your power of imagination and creativity balanced by your empirical experiences and value system.

III. Finally, **DISCUSSION** or **INFORMATIVE** questions used exclusively in group settings are designed expressly to evidence your communication skills by encouraging group interaction. You may be expected to critique a passage, comment on a current event, react to another competitor's statement, or simply convey your thoughts and/or feelings about a controversial topic. Although what you say is important, be aware that you might not be judged more or less favorably based on the position you choose to take. Instead, *how* you present your views may be the important factor under observation and consideration.

Do you explain and support your statements? Do you articulate your thoughts well? Are your thoughts organized and convincing? Do you demonstrate your command of English? Do you look confident? How are your presentation skills, verbal and non-verbal? In such situations, it is also imperative that you diffuse emotional bombs, remaining calm, controlled, and non-defensive. Above all, avoid dominating the discussion or allowing yourself be "dominated."

As a rule of thumb, go with the flow. If the majority of your interview group is firing comments at a fast pace, it may not be wise to sit quietly "waiting for your turn". However, it may be wise to select your comments carefully and speak sparingly for dramatic effect or contrast. The bottom line: think strategically. What position or approach will have the greatest impact on your observers/listeners? If you find that yours is the only voice that everyone continually hears, pause and slow down! He or she that speaks loudest, fastest, or the most, does not always win the prize. Be intelligent and give intelligent input. Practice controlling and managing your level of assertiveness.

WHAT JUDGES LOOK FOR DURING INTERVIEWS

By the interview stage of the competition, rest assured that the judges are significantly impressed with you from what they have read in your combined application, essay, letters of recommendation, and activity list. Now they anticipate meeting you in person and will be searching for that one quality (or several qualities) that sets you a notch above the rest of the applicants.

Recognize, however, that it is not always the most altruistic, standard, "give-them-what-they-want-to-hear" response that elicits favorable reactions in an interview. Honesty, sincerity, creativity, and the *manner* in which you present your answers can speak louder than an over-eager response. These attributes are acquired skills that must be diligently learned, practiced, and lived so that you can deliver responses spontaneously, naturally and with self-confidence. Every word you utter during an interview must reflect an appropriate articulation of meaningful value.

H I G H L I G H T

"She Only Said One Thing"

A nationally recognized bank sponsors a scholarship in the form of a debate on current issues. Panels of judges both observe and ask questions, and the contest happens in three stages: (1)Locally where high schools select their best students to compete; (2)regionally where winners of the local contests compete; and, (3) nationally in a "final" competition, where regional winners vie for the top award.

One student reported, "The competition was fierce at the local level, with every contestant striving to dominate the discussion, forcefully advocating his or her ideas, and trying to have the last word. I won the local and regional contests which seemed to encourage maximum verbal participation. However, at the final competition, I took second place to a student who contributed only one brief comment midway through the debate (which lasted an hour). Although she only said one thing, she timed it perfectly and presented it so masterfully that it changed the course of the entire discussion."

The moral of the story: remember remember to be adaptable, flexible, and aware of the level and type of communication required in every situation.

BEFORE THE INTERVIEW

Dress professionally. Prepare to make a good first impression with your clothes. As soon as you walk into the interview room, judges are already quietly scrutinizing your appearance in their minds, forming that important "first impression" consciously or unconsciously. Your hair, nails, teeth, shoes, and socks should be neatly groomed. Some individuals maintain that you should dress like your interviewers (assuming you are able to ascertain or estimate with some degree of confidence how they will dress ahead of time).

Generally speaking, your outfit should be pleasant and enhance your personality. It should not be distracting or more noticeable than you in any way. To achieve this effect, it is probably well to wear simple, tasteful business suits or dresses, and to stick with solid colors or small patterns. Avoid large, loud multi-colored patterns, extreme accessories, and heavy make-up (unless applying for a fashion scholarship!).

Some pundits have suggested that wearing red is a "power color." However, abandon those jeans! Well-pressed shirts with crisp, clean suits and ties are acceptable for most scholarship interviews. If you have a pin or tie-tac of which you are especially proud (Eagle Scout Pin, Scholarship Pin, club pin, etc.), now might be the perfect time to display it. But the bottom line is: Think carefully when considering your physical appearance and what you will wear during interviews.

Plan logistics ahead of time. Consider preparing for the interview in the following ways:

- Check to see that you have the correct address and directions on how to get there. Consult a map if necessary.

- Arrange for transportation with your parents, teachers, neighbors, or friends if you are not driving yourself.

- Review your copy of the application, reading carefully your activities and the essay(s) which you may have written.

- Bring some notepaper and a pen/pencil, extra money for parking, meals, or gasoline; a copy of the application you submitted; your personal portfolio; and any other specific item(s) requested for the interview.

DURING THE INTERVIEW

Introduce yourself. If the interview setting is appropriate, you may offer to shake hands with the interviewer(s) when you are introduced, gripping firmly to communicate your self-confidence, and then *clearly* state your name. As a general rule, you should always remain standing until you are asked or invited to sit down.

Maintain positive body language. Kinesics and proxemics have long fascinated behavioral psychologists. Kinesics is the study of body language, and proxemics is the study of the influence of body proximity relative to others. You have probably noticed in many non-western cultures where individuals talking to each other casually may be standing much closer than you might normally feel comfortable in doing. In some cultures, it may be characteristic to use lots of hand gestures when speaking or to speak almost argumentatively during friendly conversation—as a matter of fact, these cultural speech patterns can become quite complex.

We, as human beings, use more than words to communicate. During communication or interaction in an interview environment, our unspoken body language can have a powerfully positive and effective impact on our overall presentation if we remember a few simple guidelines and tips.

When sitting, remember to sit up *straight* near the edge of the chair and plant your feet squarely on the floor. This forces your arms and hands to fall naturally into your lap and indicates comfortable self-assurance even when you are nervous. Leaning slightly forward with the top half of your body also expresses "enthusiasm" and is more convincing sometimes than verbalizing aloud, "I am enthusiastic!" Although this may sound foolish, practicing sitting is *extremely important*. Sitting properly can help you release nervous energy, a key precursor to successful verbal communication.

If you are nervous, here is a formula to help you through the interview and that incorporates many of the principles just discussed:

✐ **SHOW UP EARLY.** As previously mentioned, we recommend that you arrive at least 10 minutes early for an interview. However, some students prefer to arrive a half hour to an hour before any interview. Plan cushion time for parking, finding interview locations, traffic conditions, and the unexpected. Allowing for sufficient time before an interview avoids the frustration and panic that a last minute rush can cause.

✐ **GET GROUNDED.** Say in your mind that this chair and this piece of floor is MY floor and MY chair. Claim it. Be assured of yourself and your position. This attitude releases nervous energy.

✐ **GET RELAXED.** Calm yourself. Stand or sit naturally. Take a deep breath and let it out slowly.

✐ **GET FOCUSED.** One interviewer calls this concept contracting; that is, clarifying in your own mind the purpose of the meeting, what you want to convey, and why you are there. Focus on the situation "here and now." Gather your thoughts. Pause to think. Look into your interviewer's eyes.

✐ **MAKE CONTACT.** To alleviate any initial intimidation, ask yourself, "What is it about that person or these interviewers that I really like?" If you can convince yourself that you like your interviewer(s), you will act as if they are friends, not interrogators. Stay positive instead of negative. Smile during your initial introduction.

✐ **GET CONCRETE.** As you answer questions, make sure your communications come from the heart, empirical experiences, and genuine feelings. Be sincere. This posture helps you to project an appearance of certainty, not hesitation. Even though a particular interview may warrant an academic approach, we believe that most judges generally prefer "real" people who express theselves in a natural, unpretentious manner.

✐ **CHECK.** Restate and confirm questions if they are unclear or if you need to digest what is being asked in your own mind.

✐ **GET CLOSURE.** Many interviews end with a solicitation to the scholarship candidate for any questions or additional comments not covered during the interview. Always have prepared in the back of your mind some thing to say or ask so that you are not caught off-guard. Leave the interview *smiling*.

An accomplished student violinist related that when he was learning to perform, he discovered that there was a whole separate body of skills to master in addition to just playing his instrument—a set of rules called "showmanship." To master showmanship for playing the violin in an orchestra, this student learned that when standing or sitting, the left foot is to be placed further out that the right foot, that the body should be angled in a certain manner relative to both the musician's chair and the music stand, and that the musician should always sit on the edge of his or her chair. He was also instructed that these "rules" not only create a more aesthetically appealing pose for spectators in the audience but also facilitates better control, focus, and release of energy.

The same analogy holds true on the "stage" of interviewing. There is a whole body of rules to know and apply (hopefully as second nature) beyond mere verbal oration. One must position the body properly so as to focus energy in the most effective manner possible, appear pleasant, and communicate effectively. Avoid shaking your legs or feet and twiddling your fingers. Avoid anything that will detract from your verbal presentation. Practice so that these behaviors become a habit.

T H O U G H T

We are what we repeatedly do.

Excellence, then, is not an act, but a habit.

—*Aristotle*

As already mentioned, a key principle in our formula for interviewing success is to *look frequently* at the interviewer and establish eye contact every few seconds (but do not constantly stare into his or her eyes). In so doing, you assure interviewers that you are concentrating on what they are saying, and more importantly, that what you have to say is significant.

Use appropriate hand expressions to emphasize a point, always ensuring that your hand movements are well controlled and appropriate for the point(s) you are trying to convey. Avoid overusing hand motions, but rather, use them tastefully. In this manner, they can become powerful tools for effective communication.

Remember to smile! A smile communicates warmth and genuine sincerity. Smile freely.

Avoid fidgeting, "wringing" your hands, bouncing your knees up and down, tapping your feet, or in many cases, even crossing your legs (except at the ankles for ladies), as these gestures may detract from the overall effectiveness of your presentation. *And avoid chewing gum!*

Now, imagine that you are one of several judges interviewing a whole group of finalists. Read the following examples from true interview scenarios and write what nonverbal messages are being communicated:

1. As the finalists enter the room, one particular finalist immediately smiles upon seeing the judges.

MESSAGE:_____

_____

2. A shy young lady slowly enters the room, shuffles to her seat, and looks down at her shoes, waiting silently for the judges to speak.

MESSAGE:_____

_____

3. During the course of the interview, you notice that one of the more talkative finalists keeps tapping his finger and looking at his watch while others are speaking.

MESSAGE:_____

_____

4. When asked a question, one finalist wrinkles his brows, frowns, and heaves a big sigh.

MESSAGE:_____

_____

5. One young lady is sitting on the edge of her chair and is looking directly into your eyes.

MESSAGE:_____

_____

Your impressions may sound like the following: A smiling finalist immediately indicates his genuine enthusiasm at being present (#1). Shyness, on the other hand, shows nothing but a lack of self-confidence (#2). A fidgeting finalist is either impatient with his competitors, bored with their comments, or concerned more about time (#3), while a finalist who contorts his face at every question may be confused by questions or find them too difficult to answer (#4). A finalist who looks directly at the judge is interested, confident, and thinking carefully about the questions asked (#5).

Listen carefully. Remember, judges are leading the interview, and you will be responding. Listen patiently until a question is completely asked before responding. Focus on *what* is being asked and give specific answers accordingly. Many times, scholarshippers are so preoccupied worrying about what to say next that important details of a question are often overlooked, and they are then left to provide less than ideal responses.

Practice effective voice techniques. In our experience, the most powerful interviewee is one who uses a combination of specific voice characteristics to convey enthusiasm, excitement, and personality. To do this, simply vary the **tone** and **speed** of your voice to match your message and emotions. For instance, lowering the voice volume and slowing the speed at which you speak creates a "serious or calm" effect, while speaking without any change in pitches is "monotone," and hence, BORING. In some cases, a louder voice can project enthusiasm, excitement, and eagerness, while in other cases it could appear boisterous or irreverent. Appropriate voice control for the situation at hand is a key to effective interviews.

Practice the following introduction, presenting yourself eight times aloud, using the suggested voice characteristics, and notice how they can affect your message. Then, use a *combination* of speeds and tones. You may want to record this on a tape recorder and play it back for evaluation purposes.

INTRODUCING YOURSELF:

Good morning! My name is (your first and last name) from (your high school) in (your city).

SPEED:	TONE:
1. Fast	1. High pitched
2. Slow	2. Low pitched
3. Moderate	3. Loud volume
	4. Soft volume
	5. Medium volume

Express your thoughts and feelings clearly. Articulate your words, pronouncing every syllable clearly. There is little need to embellish, so keep diction and word choice simple. If you have a tendency to mumble or slur your words, consciously begin moving your lips, tongue, cheeks, and jaw in over-exaggerated motions as you speak. One student went so far as to even read out loud to himself for 15 minutes every night before going to bed. The more you enunciate, the better prepared you will be for an interview. Try to speak in complete sentences, not partial phrases. A lot can also be learned about proper oral communication by watching and imitating your favorite television news anchor.

Use assertive statements. Act and sound as if you already knew you were going to win! Phrases such as "I know" or "I'm confident" or "I must", sound factual and are cue "confidence" phrases that evoke a positive, "WOW! That's great!" response from the listener. On the other hand, phrases such as "I think" or "I'm pretty sure" or "as far as I know" are phrases that sound doubtful, apologetic, or faithless and evokes a mere "Oh, how nice..." response from the listener. Consider these examples:

LESS EFFECTIVE	MORE EFFECTIVE
"I guess you could say I'm a pretty good athlete. At least, that's what my coach always tells me!"	"I believe community service has been vital in the development of my personal traits and leadership abilities."
"As far as I know, the new Student Crisis Club is the best thing to come onto campus so far, and I'm glad to have been a part of it."	"I know from personal experience that the new Student Crisis Club has performed a crucial role in helping disturbed students on campus."
"Yeah, I've learned a lot playing sports."	"As an athlete, I have enjoyed developing my talents in the area of basketball and soccer while learning about teamwork."
"Gosh, students can really get out and do some good in the world these days."	"In order to develop effective leadership abilities, students must serve and become an integral part of their communities."

Always accentuate the positive. You can always turn a negative around into a positive. So, stay away from mentioning the negatives. Although it might be tempting to blurt out whatever comes to your mind at first, you may end up hurting your credibility in the end if you appear negative to your listeners.

LESS EFFECTIVE	MORE EFFECTIVE
Interviewer: Which courses did you like best or least? Why?	
"I generally liked all of my courses except for Calculus, which was very challenging for me. I'm not really very gifted in math."	"I appreciated my Anatomy class because it afforded me greater insight into the world of medicine, and thanks to this understanding, I've decided on my future career as a pediatrician."

Interviewer: What are your strengths and weaknesses?	
"People say that I'm a slow thinker."	"I am a methodical thinker."

Notice the difference between these two examples. The positive finalist answered the same questions as the negative finalist, but succeeded in giving a stronger impression simply because she accentuated the positive.

Demonstrate your command of English. Your command of English means remembering your "Freshman" grammar and vocabulary, while abstaining from using inappropriate slang. Moreover, eliminate the "um's", "you know", and "uh's." To find out if this plagues you, consider recording a role play with your parents, siblings, or a friend and then listening to see if your answers are cluttered with these sounds!

Be concise and specific. Judging the right length of a response in interpersonal communication can often make or break an interview. If your response takes too much time or is too detailed or lengthy, then the interviewer might have to skip other questions which could have been equally or more important in ascertaining your total character or qualifications. Moreover, the interviewer could be adversely impressed or begin to regard you as overly eager or too talkative or shallow. On the other hand, if you do not include enough substance, you could be labeled as shy, aloof, or heady.

Although judges try to look beyond superficial appearances in discerning a person's true merit, as human beings we live and govern our lives through generalities, labels, and "selective learning." In other words, the amount of verbal and non-verbal information we receive each minute of the day is so overwhelming that our brain tends to screen out all but the most important signals. And from these few signals assimilated and processed in our mind's eye, we make inferences about the entire world around us.

Although this selective learning may seem unfair, just think if we were to consciously process every stimulus or piece of information that entered our brains, we would probably never be able to make conclusive decisions or take definite actions (or sleep at night!).

In an interview environment, this principle holds especially true because judges have definite time constraints, weighty decisions to make with much at risk. The strongest cues you eschew during the interview, however few they may be, will form the basis of the judge's overall perception of you as a candidate, regardless of whether the perception actually reflects your true character or merit.

Only you can avoid giving the wrong "cues" in what you say and how you position yourself non-verbally. A well respected Canadian oil executive once told a student that, "What you say and do must not only be right, but it must appear to be right in the eyes of others insofar as possible."

WHAT IF I DON'T KNOW WHAT TO SAY OR HOW TO ANSWER A QUESTION?

Silence is not always "bad" per se. If you need to take a moment to think and gather your thoughts before responding, this is entirely appropriate. Do not feel rushed to say something flippant which you might later regret. If you really do not understand a question or are unsure of a question's meaning, asking for more clarification is certainly allowable.

In these situations, it also helps to listen to and have confidence in your *inner promptings* as well as your empirical experience. Tune into your feelings and intuition, not just logic: "The heart has its arguments with which the logic of the mind is not acquainted" (Blaise Pascal).

In addition, if at all possible, try to avoid being vague. Relate your experiences directly to questions asked. Also, try your best to offer more than just a "yes" or "no," especially when asked open-ended questions.

The questions on the following pages are intended to assist you in "rehearsing" or preparing for interviews so that you can begin to develop a wide range of possible responses in your pool of interview discussion material. However, do not become so dependent on these practice questions alone or so narrowly focused on them that you become inflexible to other questions that may be asked in the real interviewing arena.

Finally, keep track of your interview mastery skills on the "Personal Review & Progress" page that follows. This page is an assessment form to help you fine-tune specific problem areas, improve intonation techniques, overcome any poor speaking habits, or just become more comfortable with interviewing.

PRACTICE QUESTIONS

Remember, your goal should *not* be to memorize a list of "possible" questions and answers to help you through interviews. What is essential is that you become familiar enough with these three general types of questions and prepare to respond with effective and natural answers. Use the space provided below to make notes and formulate ideas about what you might say in various scenarios.

Also, remember the **"AS IF PRINCIPLE."** In other words, review scenarios in your mind first. By visualizing and working with the Practice Questions provided for you here, we are confident that your interview prowess will increase correspondingly:

I. PERSONAL

1. Tell us a little about yourself.

2. What are your educational goals?

3. What are your future career plans?

4. What motivates you to achieve and excel?

5. What is unique about you?

6. What are some of your talents?

7. What are your strengths and weaknesses?

8. What has been the most important personal quality that has contributed to your success?

9. What has been your most rewarding experience? Why?

10. What do you do in your "spare time"?

11. What hobbies do you enjoy?

12. Describe your duties as...

13. How did you become involved in (choose activity)?

14. How have these activities helped you in your life?

15. What does "leadership" mean to you?

16. What does "community service" mean to you?

17. Who is/are your role model(s) or hero(es)? Why?

18. How would you help today's youth?

19. Ten years from now, where do you want to be?

20. Who has been the most influential person in your life?

21. Describe three books you have read and what impact they have had on you.

22. Summarize your high school experience.

23. What classes did you like the best? Least?

24. In your high school career, what did you find to be the most difficult challenge to meet?

25. Describe a typical day in your life.

26. What positive impact have you had on your community (school, peers, etc.)?

27. Describe your family life.

28. Why should we give you this scholarship?

29. How do you plan to continue your leadership in college and beyond?

30. What has been your most rewarding extracurricular activity?

31. Why did you choose the particular college you will be attending?

II. HYPOTHETICAL

1. If you were selected to accompany a group of pioneers to colonize a new planet in space and allowed to bring only three books, what three books would you take with you, and why?

2. If you could be principal of your school (or mayor of city, governor of state, president of country, etc.) for a week, what changes would you make?

3. If you could interview any one in the world, who would it be and what would you ask?

4. If you could do it all over again, what would you change about your academic experience thus far?

5. When in a car, do you prefer being the driver or the passenger? Why?

6. If you could write your own epitaph, what would you say?

7. What would you do as Chief Executive Officer if your company were preparing to merge with another company?

8. If you were given one minute of broadcasting time to send a message to all the youth in this nation, what would you say?

9. If you were a rose living peacefully in a little garden when a person came along and plucked you out of your "home," how would you react?

10. If you could be in the interviewer's shoes, what characteristics and qualities would you look for in the scholarship winner?

11. Imagine you met a genie who wanted to grant you three wishes. What would you wish for?

10. If you were writing an autobiography, what would you title the book?

III. DISCUSSION/INFORMATIVE

1. What is man's greatest modern invention? Why?

2. What is your opinion of (any current event)?

3. As a product of public education, what changes would you make in the public educational system?

4. What do you consider to be the most serious issue that threatens youth today? Why?

5. What are the ethical issues of _____?

6. What do you see as trends in the new century?

7. What do you consider more important in today's world—logic or emotion?

8. What do you think educational leaders need to do to improve education?

9. Discuss some social issues that will need to be addressed in order to ensure continued societal progress over the next 10 years.

10. Agree or Disagree on political issues (health care, use of laboratory animals, traditional teaching, medical insurance, taxes, science and medicine, applied and fine arts, humanities). Explain why.

PERSONAL REVIEW & PROGRESS PAGE

I. ACTIVITY:

❑ DO THE SAMPLE QUESTIONS

❑ RECORD YOUR RESPONSES;

❑ LISTEN TO AND CRITIQUE RECORDING

❑ DO ROLE PLAYS WITH A PARENT OR FRIEND

❑ VIDEOTAPE A ROLE PLAY; WATCH
   AND CRITIQUE IT

❑ TALK TO YOURSELF IN THE MIRROR

II. Interviewing skills at which I am GOOD:

_____   _____

_____   _____

_____   _____

III. Interviewing skills that I need to DEVELOP:

SKILL: HOW I PLAN TO DO IT: Done:

1. _____   a. _____   ❑

                    b. _____   ❑

2. _____   a. _____   ❑

                    b. _____   ❑

3. _____   a. _____   ❑

                    b. _____   ❑

THE POSITIVE MENTAL ATTITUDE

7

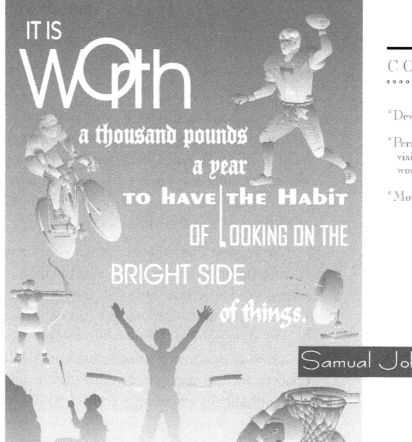

THE POSITIVE MENTAL ATTITUDE

Empower yourself with an attitude of success

Correct attitudes toward scholarshipping should begin with a clear personal vision of yourself achieving success! Dismiss negative thoughts or feelings of inadequacy because the opportunities and possibilities are limitless. Envision yourself as winning—many athletes can attest to the power of positive thinking and of visualizing success in their mind's eye.

We suggest that you *do not worry yourself unnecessarily!* Having undergone this "fire of tribulation" repeatedly ourselves, we know how stressful, intense, and competitive the scholarship application process can be, as well as how lonely and directionless scholarship seekers may feel on more than one occasion. Of course, we congratulate you on your concern for the success of your future academic career, but we emphatically encourage you not to worry—there is a difference!

Concern creates healthy stimulation and a sense of urgency to work both hard and smart, but worrying serves to dim your enthusiasm and defeat your vital inner drive and spirit. Never be afraid of losing. . . or winning! Babe Ruth struck out 1,330 times before reaching 714 home runs. Win or lose, the scholarship experience, itself, becomes priceless.

What ultimately decides whether your quest remains positive or negative is your own personal reaction, or rather, how you choose to allow winning and losing to affect your attitudes and emotions. If you turn "proud and heady" after winning a scholarship (even if you really deserved to win) you will have won nothing of true worth. On the other hand, if you become depressed, discouraged, or intimidated after losing a scholarship contest, even if you were perhaps the most qualified, then you will have missed the point as well.

In scholarshipping, as in life, winners are those whose characters become increasingly refined and perfected through each contest process. Win or lose, they evaluate their experiences and assimilate into their personality those lessons which further their opportunities for individual growth. Winners naturally attract scholarship awards because they are constant, genuine, real people who work hard and know how to endure. They invest and believe in themselves; they realize that the duty of life is to progress.

Approach the art of scholarshipping with this attitude, and you will automatically become a winner. Don't worry about your weaknesses. Improve them as much as possible, but then concentrate on accentuating your strengths. Remember, you are only competing with less than 5% of the entire population of high school graduates. Why? Because, as mentioned earlier, while everyone wants to be successful, only 5% are ever willing to work for it. What we strive to achieve becomes easier to achieve because our ability to achieve increases as we continue to achieve! Remember that to progress, we must first try—and try again if necessary! Above all else, the word "quit" should have little meaning in your vocabulary.

KEEP YOURSELF POSITIVE AND MOTIVATED!

Be cheerful. Practice happiness—the real "you" shows in your face, your eyes, and in your posture. Watch motivational movies, observe positive people, surround yourself with positive company. Carry with you or display in your room several of your favorite motivational thoughts. Memorize them if you can. Think about them often. Make the application of them in your life second nature. Here are only two of several favorite uplifting quotes in particular that constantly remind us to have a positive mental attitude:

PRESS ON.

Nothing in the world can take the place of PERSISTENCE.

TALENT will not.

Nothing is more common than unsuccessful men with talent.

GENIUS will not.

Unrewarded genius is almost a proverb.

EDUCATION will not.

The world is full of educated derelicts.

PERSISTENCE AND DETERMINATION

are alone omnipotent.

—Calvin Coolidge

These words by Theodore Roosevelt should be engraved upon the minds of all courageous men and women who dare to achieve excellence.

It is not the critic who counts, not the man who points out how the strong man stumbled, or where the doer of deeds could have done them better. The credit belongs to the man who is actually in the arena; whose face is marred by dust and sweat and blood; who strives valiantly; who comes short again and again; who knows the great enthusiasms, the great devotions, and spends himself in a worthy cause; who at best knows in the end the triumph of high achievement; and who, at the worst, if he fails, at least fails while daring greatly, so that his place shall never be with those cold and timid souls who know neither victory nor defeat.

It matters little what socio-economic circumstances surround you, or what obstacles lie in your path to success. Except for yourself, *no one* can take away your agency to be and act as the best individual you think possible. Those who do not conquer sabotaging thoughts of fear and low self-esteem rob themselves of a powerful inner-source of comfort and confidence during times when they most desperately need it. Inner strength and confidence command attention—it's that simple. Some have come to term this elusive quality as "charisma."

So, how do we acquire that level of self-assurance which automatically elicits the respect of others? We have already mentioned some of the tools to appear poised, but true and lasting poise or gracefulness can only be developed when one is first at *peace* with himself or herself. You must be integrated internally within your own *spirit*. You must know where you stand, what you believe, who you are. This type of inner strength does not come in the crowd or from the classroom. It comes from self-understanding, quiet meditation and frequent introspection, by developing and adhering to a firm set of personal values. What is your personal mission in life? What are your core values and set of life principles? In religious terms, we might ask, "in what do you have faith?" These are the essential weapons you must carry with you in order to endure through the challenging experiences of scholarshipping.

Whatever your set of beliefs or core values in life, religious or otherwise (and we hope you do have them!), you should be able to stand up courageously and declare them with conviction in both word and action. You must live true to your ideals.

A mother and her young child were strolling along a pathway one day, and the mother pointed to a large rose bush with many flowers in bloom. She said, "See what lovely flowers these are!" Some days later, her child saw another rose bush with flower buds that were not yet open. He wanted the flowers to be just as beautiful as the ones they had seen days before, so he proceeded to open each petal one by one only to find that the flower fell apart instead of becoming beautiful. He went home and related this episode to his mother and asked, "Why couldn't I make them as beautiful as the ones we saw the other day?" The mother replied, "Because God works from the inside out." In other words, great *inner* character precedes *outward* excellence in accomplishment.

As Stephen Covey, renowned leadership consultant and author, has observed: "Many people with secondary greatness—that is, social recognition for their talents—lack primary greatness or goodness in their character. . . . It is character that communicates most eloquently. As Emerson once put it, 'What you are shouts so loudly in my ears that I cannot hear what you say.'" [1]

---

[1] *The Seven Habits of Highly Effective People* (Simon and Schuster). Copyright © 1989 by Stephen R. Covey. All rights reserved. Used with permission of the author.

In short, to become an effective scholarshipper, you must not only master the tools and techniques of good scholarshipping but also foster great character. Then, whether or not you actually win the award, you have already achieved true success!

BROADEN YOUR VISION

Besides developing a solid, genuinely wholesome character, another dimension of acquiring the proper attitudes towards scholarshipping rests in establishing a long term vision. What is your vision of the future? What is your *real* purpose in scholarshipping?

The following worksheets are designed to help you look within yourself and create a personal long-term vision and mission. As you complete these worksheets, refer back to them often, revise them as necessary, and as time progresses use them to remind yourself of your personal objectives whenever the going may get tough during the scholarshipping process.

With this "bird's eye" perspective constantly before you, you will receive added motivation to fulfill your goals.

**PERSONAL LONG TERM VISION
AND PLANNING WORKSHEET**

Objectives:

- Develop a vision of your preferred future and a snap shot of your immediate high school career and beyond.

- Determine how it will guide you personally and how it will affect your family and your scholarshipping endeavors.

- Define the drivers and potential barriers to achieving your vision.

- Prepare a set of goals that will move you toward achieving your vision and help you throughout the scholarshipping process.

Groundrules:

✏ Don't commit to something unless you really mean it.

✏ Let go of assumptions about the way things have been in the past.

✏ Forget about any constraints or limits.

Process:

1) Create a Personal Vision/Mission Statement

Describes where you're going, what you want to look or be like, clarifies your purpose, defines what is important for you to focus on in the scholarshipping process.

2) Decide how to use your Vision/Mission Statement

Integrate it into your natural approach to daily decision-making and your scholarshipping activities.

3) Eliminate Barriers and Obstacles

Understand what is driving you toward your vision and what may be standing in the way of success.

4) Prepare a 3 year plan

Build a plan that enables you to focus yourself, train, and measure progress toward successful scholarshipping.

1) Create a Personal Vision/Mission Statement:

Purpose: To formally articulate your personal identity, purpose, and vision to which you are inwardly committed.

Process: Create a snapshot of how you see yourself and circumstances 3-5 years down the road

Groundrules: Step away from what is for a moment and think about what could be. Imagine how you would like things to be and/or how you would like yourself to be (in college, your profession, etc.)

In your snapshot consider:

✐ What does your preferred future look like in college and beyond?_____

_____

_____

✐ What are you doing then and there_____

_____

_____

✐ How are you doing it?_____

_____

_____

✐ What are the central focus points in your life?_____

_____

_____

✐ How do you want others (peers, family, friends) to view you; what does it feel like?_____

_____

_____

✐ What would you like to say you accomplished?_____

_____

_____

✐ How are you different than you are today?_____

_____

_____

✐ What can you continually strive to improve?_____

_____

_____

Key information related to developing your Vision/Mission statement:

1) Your religious or core spiritual beliefs.

2) Any information from past or future personal or family goals.

NOTE: Be sure that you make your vision specific enough to guide you in tough situations (i.e. a tough interview question), but general enough to allow you room to exercise your agency in responding to challenges that confront you. Also, share your vision only with others who will help you in achieving it (i.e. your parents, family, and very close friends).

2) Decide How to Use Your Vision/Mission Statement:

✎ How can your Vision Statement help you in your day-to-day scholarshipping activities?_____

_____

_____

✎ What should you start doing differently as a result of this Vision statement?_____

_____

_____

✎ How will you remember it and keep it foremost in your mind? _____

_____

_____

3) Eliminate Barriers and Obstacles:

✎ What is keeping you from moving toward the realization of your Vision/Mission and winning scholarships? _____

_____

_____

✐ What are the drivers that can help you realize your Vision/Mission and win scholarships? _____

_____

_____

✐ What Forces/Drivers do you need to eliminate or strengthen to allow you to move toward your Vision and successful scholarshipping? _____

_____

_____

✐ What two or three actions would have the biggest impact in helping you move forward? _____

_____

_____

4) Prepare a 3 Year Semi-Annual Plan:

Purpose: To translate the Vision/Mission Statement into Goals and Objectives that focus your priorities and scholarshipping activities over the next three years

Data needed: Your vision/mission statement and list of barriers and obstacles.

Process:

1) Look at your Vision; what are the top few items you need to focus on related to scholar shipping? Prioritize them.

2) With respect to these prioritized items, what specifically will you accomplish in the next several months to move you closer to your Vision? Write them down and assign dates.

3) Brainstorm for additional ideas/objectives and build them into your 3 Year Plan.

Remember that drafting your Mission Statement is not just an academic exercise. Writing it down and reviewing it frequently allows you to see if it really reflects what you have in mind for the long term, and it gives meaning to your scholarship pursuit. Developing a personal vision of where you want to be in the future not only helps you weather the minor storms in the present which scholarshipping can bring, but also forms an important basis for developing true leadership skills, a pre-requisite for any scholarship for which you may apply, as has been discussed in previous chapters.

> "Where there is no vision, the people perish...."
>
> —Proverbs 29:18

As you complete the vision/mission worksheet described in this chapter, take time to meditate, ponder, and think in order to receive inspiration. A good time for this activity is in the morning when your mind is fresh. Chase away gloom or depressive thoughts. They are unconducive to the develop-ment of visions and missions—and to good scholarshipping! As you begin to experience compelling impulses, enlighten-ing thoughts, or ideas flowing into your mind, we are confi-dent that you will feel inspired and imbued with knowledge and that you will be directed to right actions and attitudes, especially toward scholarshipping.

Quite simply, your vision is the overriding spirit behind the scholarshipping process, the "why" you are doing this in the first place. It will form the basis of the kind of attitude that you should possess in the achievement of scholarshipping success.

THE EXTRA MILE ATTITUDE

Scholarshipping involves directed effort that is calculated, planned, well thought-out, and not compelled by circum-stances. Directed effort is internally motivated and consists of objectives and goals directed toward a purpose. Directed effort necessitates an extra-mile attitude, going beyond the routine, moving out of the status quo, and therefore creating and having new and challenging experiences which lead to growth and development. This is the type of positive attitude you must have to become a successful scholarshipper.

Remember, however, not to become so rigid in your goals that scholarshipping evolves into an obsession or an end in itself, but rather, treat the scholarship process as a means to obtaining something greater, a higher education and more opportunities to become useful in life. Also, do not become so glued to your goals that there exists little room for change as time progresses and as your scholarshipping experiences mature.

Finally, scholarshipping skills demand a particular, unique mind-set and group of character traits which will assist you in your efforts. Throughout the course, we have described successful leadership attitudes, principles, and character traits in great detail. They have been offered as food for thought in your preparations for a successful scholarshipping experience, as well as academic career. Above all, be positive. Be true to yourself. Have fun!

Inspirational Quotes

Collect your favorite motivational quotes in the following spaces, and read them often to help empower yourself with an attitude of success!

ESPECIALLY FOR PARENTS

8

Definition of a good parent or manager *is one who says,*

"**You** **can become** **whatever it is** **you seriously want** **to become;**

My job *is to help you become it.*"

Harry Levinson

CONTENTS

○ ○ ○ ○ ○ ○ ○ ○ ○ ○ ○ ○ ○ ○ ○ ○ ○

ESPECIALLY FOR PARENTS

Empower yourself with an attitude of success

When my husband and I were first married 40 years ago, we made several goals, one of which was to see that all of our children received a college education. In those days, the world seemed rosy and the future held a plethora of opportunities for anyone who subscribed to the American work ethic. Who could have guessed that our national economy would someday decay to its current chaotic condition and that convulsive socio-political events would create massive turmoil and uncertainty well into the new Century.

Today, unemployment threatens to shatter the dreams of countless young couples and families who have developed goals just as my husband and I did many years ago. Even natural disasters are taking their toll in disrupting the lives of decent, hard-working, and honest people everywhere.

The purpose of this chapter, however, is *not* to reinforce the negatives that we see happening around us, but rather to re-affirm the simple faith and hope which keeps American families moving forward and upward in spite of all odds. I am convinced, without equivocation, that it IS possible for a single wage earner family from a middle–to low-income neighborhood with four or more children of college age to send every one of them to a four-year private or public university! My husband and I did it, and we did it through the medium of a wonderful, magical phenomenon called *scholarships*.

Your task—the hard part—rests in preparing your child to actually *win* the scholarships when the time comes for him or her to compete. In his popular book, *The Seven Habits of Highly Effective People*, Stephen Covey argued that what the world needs today are individuals who exhibit the "Character Ethic" rather than the "Personality Ethic."[1] He suggested that society has become increasingly appearance-centered, superficial, and "personality oriented" (Personality Ethic).

On the other hand, those who seem to find true happiness in life and who achieve lasting success in its deepest sense are individuals who become integrated in terms of their values, core beliefs, and personal character (Character Ethic).

The confidence of these successful individuals is inner-directed rather than outward-directed. Their sense of self-worth stems from peace of mind rather than material possessions, status, affluence, or peer pressure. Hence, we have tried to direct our efforts in this workbook to the development of more than a few trite rules-of-thumb and trendy techniques. We have also tried to share *concepts* and *principles* that, when adapted to situation-specific needs and integrated in one's character, can produce above-average results in scholarshipping as well as in other areas of life.

We have included this chapter because we believe that you, as a parent or parents, play the *most crucial* role in fostering sound character in your children The atmosphere created at home plants seeds of greatness or failure in the hearts of young people, and the type of family environment which parents cultivate can determine in large measure the degree of their child's success as they enter mainstream society.

We have observed that what students learn (or do not learn) at home often separates those who win scholarships from those who merely compete. In fact, I would dare say that the family experiences my own children received in our "home laboratory"—their social graces, worldview, discipline, and personal values—became fodder for critical scholarship interviews, formal debates, and application essays much more frequently than any academic knowledge or training they received at school.

Furthermore, as a parent, you are often able to recognize the difference between manifestations of superficiality versus "good character" more clearly than your child. Because of your empirical experiences, you know your child well and

---

[1] *The Seven Habits of Highly Effective People* (Simon and Schuster). Copyright © 1989 by Stephen R. Covey. All rights reserved. Used with permission of the author.

can usually see further down life's road than he or she can. Therefore, it becomes your responsibility and blessing to warn, coach, and encourage them to strive for greatness by teaching and modeling successful character traits and habits.

Rest assured, we do not intend to dictate how you should run your family (by no means have we been flawless parents ourselves). Yet, there seem to be some universally applicable traditions that we have attempted to practice in our home and which our children can attest have influenced them positively in the pursuit of scholarships (as well as in other areas of their lives). For what they are worth, we would like to share these practices with you:

Daily, Regular, Non-Structured Communication Sessions

Even before my children started kindergarten, we began to cultivate within them a desire to or habit of communicating regularly during daytime hours so that when they entered school, it was only natural for this pattern to continue. As our children arrived home from classes each day, and before they began their homework, I would drop everything—cooking, phone calls, cleaning, *everything*—to sit with them and give them undivided attention while they recounted to me their day's activities.

During our discussions, I took as much time as necessary to listen, comfort, counsel, correct, discuss, laugh with, or praise my children depending on the situation. Sometimes the discussions would last a few minutes, but sometimes they would last for hours (occasionally at the expense of dinner and other activities).

By the time my children entered college, the practice of daily "rap" sessions had become such an ingrained tradition that they would think nothing of calling home long distance to tell me about what was happening in their lives, not withstanding my increasingly hefty phone bills! Many of my children's teachers at school eventually asked how I was able to "get" my children to excel and achieve so much, whereupon I would share this simple but powerful stratagem (I consider this one of my greatest pearls or "secrets" to raising children just talk (and listen) to them, often!).

H I G H L I G H T

"Simple Needs"

One Northern Californian elementary school principle observed that immediately after the devastating 1994 earthquake in Los Angeles, his school's health office received a record number of visits from students. What was unusual was that *none* of the complaints were related to physical injuries normally acquired on the playground. After a careful investigation, school officials concluded that even though the children did not physically feel the impact of the Southern California quake, simply having heard about the disaster invoked insecurity and fear within them—they needed direct attention and reassurance.

Likewise, scholarshipping can present a psychologically scary experience. There will come times when your children need your direct attention, a listening ear, and willing reassurance. You must have the capacity to be there when they need you, to understand with your heart, and to feel that which they might not be able to adequately express.

Family Evenings or Family Council

Another practice that fostered unity and mutual support within our family as my children were growing up was to hold weekly "family evening" or "family council" meetings. At the same time and place every week (normally Monday nights in our family), everyone gathered together to evaluate events of the past week, review the family's schedule for the upcoming week, receive guidance and counsel, resolve problems, talk of current events, and most importantly, enjoy each other's company uninterrupted.

Doing this on a reasonably consistent basis helped us receive valuable input concerning our children's needs so that we could plan ahead as parents. We also arranged ways to help and participate in upcoming activities or projects. We profited greatly from the exchange of ideas and thoughts. And we truly learned how to care for and support each other.

During their high school experience, when my children were constantly rehearsing with the band or performing with various orchestras at night or attending long club meetings, trying to find enough time to go to the public library before the doors were locked and do research for a paper or a book report was always sure to become a nightmare. Instead, we would discuss our children's assignments during family home evenings, and then as appropriate, we would plan how each of us could best help.

Sometimes it meant keeping our eyes open for journal or newspaper articles. If there were articles and ideas that might be useful, I would mark it or set it aside as a possible reference. At other times, flexibility was the key. That meant taking a trip to pick up materials that our children needed while they were at rehearsals or other activities. In any case, many potential crises situations were avoided because of this "collective cooperation."

True, each child should be—and was entirely responsible for—completing their homework and assignments themselves. But it is equally important to realize that helpful support can also mean executing good judgment and doing what is reasonable within the time constraints allowed. Sometimes, that may entail a little extra time, money, and gas on our part as a parent or parents to pick up books from the library or buy poster board and markers for a presentation.

Rest assured that the lasting benefits of your effort to simply meet as a family once a week will definitely be worth it! The synergy created by family solidarity is an unparalleled secret of scholarshipping success.

FAMILY INVOLVEMENT IN COMMUNITY AND SCHOOL EVENTS

Volunteerism is a great key to teaching your child the traits and experiences he or she needs to give them confidence and depth of character in pursuing scholarships. In hindsight, helping my children to worry less about how successful they were and more about how useful they could be was an essential ingredient in their ultimate scholarship success.

Help your child *begin community and school involvement early*. Many, if not most, scholarship committees look for *depth* of involvement as well as *breadth*. In other words, our experience has shown that the students who seem to exhibit consistency of community-mindedness will almost always win over others who may have had a variety of impressive activities but for very short durations of time and with very shallow participation.

Starting the habit of volunteerism is easier when young, and people are more forgiving! However, if your child is approaching the critical scholarshipping timetable (Junior or Senior year), all is not lost—*start now*!

I believe that the most precious two assets you can provide your child during the scholarshipping years is your time and understanding. Regardless of whether you are a busy executive or a bed-ridden invalid, you must give your child both *quantity* and *quality* with respect to your time. And the earlier in life that you can devote this kind of time to your child, the better off (and more successful at scholarshipping) they will likely become.

Finally, a wealth of research by psychologists could probably be cited to support our contentions, but the point is simple: the more security children feel at home, the more courageous and successful they will feel in venturing outside the home. And as their successes multiply outside the home, I firmly believe that bonds inside the home can become increasingly strengthened in turn. Your support at home will reinforce the positive aspects of life as well as help your child endure difficult and sometimes disappointing trials during the scholarshipping process.

H I G H L I G H T

"Making Real Opportunities"

One young man is an excellent concert violinist and has performed with numerous orchestras. Many parents of younger children just starting out on the violin have asked this violinist's parents for tips on how they were able to motivate their son to play so well. One favorite response is that they simply volunteered their son to perform! Some surprised parent(s) would respond that their children aren't "that good" yet, but this young violinist's wise parents would say, "He didn't become good and then perform; he became good because he was going to perform!"

When this young man was volunteered to perform, his parents didn't have to force him to practice—he naturally wanted to practice because his own neck was "on the line"! After experiencing minor successes (because adults are good at giving children positive reinforcement whether deserved or not), he was motivated to practice even harder. Soon, rather than telling him to practice, this violinist's parents had to tell him NOT to practice because he was waking up the neighbors! If there are no opportunities for your children to become involved through volunteerism, create some, or better yet, help them to create the opportunities—this reflects well on their leadership abilities when included in a scholarship application.

EPILOG

As you can tell, I have a rather straight-forward communication style. In my experience, that type of approach seems to work the best when relating to young people. Besides, at my age, it comes naturally! I hope that in this down-to-earth, non-nonsense (and hopefully entertaining) manner, our materials have been valuable as your student(s) prepare for scholarshipping. Beyond that, I hope you have recognized, as our family has, that these principles apply long after the scholarshipping has finished, the awards have been won, and the formal education has been obtained.

Although the world is a different place now than when I first wrote the the first edition of this manuscript, some things haven't changed. Over the years, friends, neighbors, and acquaintances have continued asking me for advice on how their children can win scholarships. Except for a few details requiring minor revisions, I have found that the principles of scholarshipping described in this "system" have remained basically the same. They are as applicable now as when I first wrote the original.

As I mentioned in the preface, all of my children have now obtained a higher education and are making their mark in various professions. Still, my desire to help young people excel during their formative "K-12" years continues to remain a deep-rooted passion.

Some have asked me how this passion began. Raising kids certainly helped, but the seeds of my interest germinated long before I was married in consequence of my own background. I grew up during wartime in a region of the world where basic survival needs of a necessity had to take priority over educational considerations. I vowed many years ago that I would do all within my power to help young people achieve their dreams of higher education because this is one of the best ways that we can avoid, or at least curtail, future socio-political and/or economic travesties that many of us have experienced in the past.

I hope you have felt my passion about the need for education through these pages and in the experiences conveyed here. More importantly, I hope that this same fire burns brightly in your own homes and family. We can only ensure a brighter future for our society by continuing to educate our youth today. The money *IS* available. My earnest desire is that everyone can be successful in claiming it.

In the scholarshipping process, I am confident that the memories you create with your child will be priceless. For example, I remember one of my children coming home from high school one afternoon extremely depressed. He had a scholarship debate the following day. As we counseled together, he recounted how some of his teachers had compared him unfavorably to his peers (who were also slated to compete in the contest). Thoughtless remarks had been made about how my son "didn't know enough," proposed "untenable ideas," and provided "weak arguments."

In a panic, my son had checked out 27 books from the school library that afternoon. He spread them all over the living room floor, and began poring through them. Finally, in utter frustration he declared, "I am *NOT* going to compete tomorrow! I don't want to let my teachers and peers see me lose and have the satisfaction of saying, 'We were right! You're not good enough. You failed!'"

I immediately dropped everything to talk with my son. I told him to put away all of the books and said that he should just be himself—his best self. That was all anyone could ask. I used every strategy I knew to build him up again (including ones I have written about in this book). I remember that by the time we were finished talking, it was 3am in the morning.

When my (drowsy but re-spirited) son left for the scholarship competition at 7am, somehow I knew inside (as only mothers can) that he would win—and he did. In fact, he kept on winning all the way to the national competition. Not only did this experience create an indelible impression upon my son, but it became a source of strength to him him thereafter whenever he was confronted with feelings of self-doubt. My hope is that the principles contained in this book will help you and your family in like manner, particularly if you are struggling with similar challenges.

Regardless of whatever happens, I trust that you and your family will have many cherished moments during the scholarshipping process. I would love to hear about them. Please let me know your successes, experiences, questions, or suggestions.

You can send them to me at P.O. Box 610986, San Jose CA 95161-0986. Although I might not be able to respond to every letter, I will read them all. Again, I wish you and yours every success during this most exciting and thrilling time in your lives. Go for it! God speed, and happy scholarshipping!

APPENDIX A

SCHOLARSHIP
SOURCES
FROM

A TO Z

This listing is intended to help you begin your scholarship search by providing a representative sample of the thousands of scholarships available today. As you read through this guide, notice the variety and breadth of scholarship types, subject areas, criteria, and sponsors. Scholarship sources are plentiful and can range from private university-sponsored stipends to programs offered by national philanthropic organizations, and from scholarships sponsored by local community groups to geographic or regional awards. A few organizations place some emphasis on financial need, while others stress exclusively merit-based criteria, and still others cater to special interests or talents. To the best of our knowledge, each of these scholarships are currently active as of the printing of this sourcebook, so you may enter any and all that apply to your situation, goals, and aspirations. More importantly, however, use this list as a springboard for finding even more scholarships in your local area and beyond. Note: Be sure to investigate the criteria for all scholarships listed herein with the actual granting organization, particularly since award availability, application guidelines, and deadlines may change from year-to-year.

American Spirit Publishing Portrait of America Scholarship

American Spirit Publishing

Attn: Portrait of America
P.O. Box 120937
Arlington, TX 76012

Phone: Not provided

Scholarships: Varies

Max. Amount: $500

Deadline: June 1

Contact: Scholarship Coordinator

Requirements: Application form, artwork

Scholarship Description: The American Spirit Publishing Portrait of America Scholarship Contest is available to students enrolled in high school. All candidates must submit an original photograph or artwork that represents their portrait of America. Students must be U.S. citizens to be eligible. Scholarship application forms are available online at the following Internet address: http://www.bestkeptsecretsforwinning.com/PortraitOfAmerica_App2007.htm

 # American Association of School Administrators

Discover Card Tribute Award
1801 N. Moore Street
Arlington, VA 22203-1730
Phone: 1-866-756-7932

Scholarships: < 300 State; 10 National

Max. Amount: $2,500

Deadline: 31 January

Contact: Scholarship Coordinator

Requirements: Reference letter, transcript
                    Application form

Scholarship Description: For high school juniors with a minimum of 2.75 GPA during grades 9 and 10. Based on academics, talents, leadership, obstacles overcome, unique endeavors, and community service. Deadlines may vary. Each state gives up to 300 awards at $2,500 each. Up to 10 national awards are granted at $25,000 each. Contact a high school counselor or AASA for application and further information. All necessary forms are usually made available by December of the preceding application year. Additional information and applications are available at: http://www.discoverfinancial.com/data/philanthropy/tribute.shtml

Bay Area Council Scholarship Program

Bay Area Council Scholarship Committee
Bay Area Family of Funds
201 California Street, Suite 1450
San Francisco, CA 94111

Phone: 415/981-6600

Scholarships: Varies

Max. Amount: $10,000

Deadline: March 26

Contact: Administrator

Requirements: Application formInterview

Scholarship Description: The Bay Area Council Scholarship Program is available to high school seniors who reside in underserved neighborhoods in a nine-county area around San Francisco. Students must plan to enroll fulltime in one of the following Bay Area schools: Mills College, Santa Clara University, Stanford University, U.C. Berkley, U.C. Davis or the University of San Francisco. Candidates must also demonstrate financial need, leadership, academic honors, and community involvement for eligibility. More information may be obtained at: http://www.bayareafamilyoffunds.org/programs/scholarship.shtml

 # California Association of Private Postsecondary Schools

CAPPS Memorial Scholarship
400 Capitol Mall, Suite 1560
Sacramento, CA 95814

Phone: 916-447-5500

Scholarships: 4

Max. Amount: $5,000 each

Deadline: April 1 - Sept 1

Contact: Scholarship Coordinator

Requirements: Special application form
                        Academic transcripts, Letter of
                        admission

Scholarship Description: For adults and graduating high school students who are enrolled in a Cosmetology/Massage/Esthetics or Allied Health program at a CAPPS member school. The scholarship is based on merit. Students do not need to demonstrate financial need. Each recipient must meet all admission requirements of the school that has pledged the scholarship. Contact the institution for specific program requirements prior to submitting application. Additional information is available at: http://cappsonline.org/scholarship.shtml

Coca-Cola Scholars Foundation, Inc.

Scholarship Information Request
PO Box 442
Atlanta, GA 30301

Phone: 404/733-5420

\# Scholarships: 50

Max. Amount: $20,000

Deadline: October 31

Contact: Scholarship Coordinator

Requirements: Reference Letter Application form, SAT/ACT/Transcripts, Resume Proof of Residency

Scholarship Description: Annual awards of four-year scholarships to outstanding high school seniors who reside in participating Coca-Cola bottlers' territories. Applicants must attend an accredited U.S. postsecondary institution. Based on academic achievement, personal merit, character, school leadership, civic and extracurricular involvement, and motivation to serve and succeed. Selection process occurs in 3 phases. Phase 1 applications are due by October 31. Semifinalists are notified in December of advancement in the program. Finalists are notified in March. Applications are distributed to counselors. Awards: 200 regional @ $4,000 each, 50 national @ $20,000 each. Applications are available via the Internet at: https://www.coca-colascholars.org/cokeWeb/jsp/scholars/Index.jsp

Dupont Science Essay Competition

Scholarship Information Request
900 Skokie Boulevard, Suite 200
Northbrook, IL 60062

Phone: 847/205-3000

\# Scholarships: Varies

Max Amount: $1,500

Deadline: February 12

Contact: Scholarship Coordinator

Requirements: Essay

Scholarship Description: Students between grades 7 and 12 who attend a public or private school in the U.S., Canada, and other territories may write an original science essay of no less than 700 and no more than 1000 words in English. Additional information and entry form available at: http://www.glcomm.com/dupont/

Educational Communications Scholarship Foundation

Scholarship Information Request
7211 Circle S Road - PO Box 149319
Austin, TX 78714-9319

Phone: 877/843-9946

\# Scholarships: Varies

Max. Amount: Up to $6,000

Deadline: Oct, Jan, Mar, May

Contact: Scholarship Coordinator

Requirements: Reference letter, SAT/ACT,
Essay, Resume, Transcripts
Financial need statement
Proof of residency
Letter of Admission

Scholarship Description: Annual award for graduating high school seniors with a GPA of "B" or better and college students with a GPA of "B+" or better. Must be U.S. citizens and attend an accredited college. Awards are based on GPA, test scores, leadership, work experience, and essay. Consideration is given to financial need as well. Forms may be downloaded from the Internet at http://www.ecisf.org/dls/whs_app_form.pdf

Elder & Leemaur Publishers

"Challenge the Experts" Scholarship
115 Garfield St. #5432
Sumas, WA 98295

Phone: Not provided

\# of Scholarships: 2

Max. Amount: $10,000

Deadline: July 1

Contact: Scholarship Coordinator

Requirements: Essay

Scholarship Description: An award available to high school juniors and seniors as well as undergraduate students in any field of study who write a 500 word essay or less addressing a topic listed on the publisher's website at http://www.elpublishers.com/content/scholarship-challengetheexperts.php

Financial Aid Center Educational Services

Frank O'Neill Memorial Scholarship
5155 N. Dysart Rd., Suite 202
#444 Litchfield Park, AZ 85340

Phone: 623-536-3332

Scholarships: 2

Max. Amount: $1,000

Deadline: December 31

Contact: Scholarship Coordinator

Requirements: Essay

Scholarship Description: This scholarship is provided to students who attend a university, trade school, technical institute or post-secondary education program. An essay of fewer than 750 words is required on a topic of the applicant's choosing. Essays are accepted online only at http://www.easyaid.com/scholarship_form.html. Winners are notified via phone and/or email.

Georgia-Pacific Foundation, Inc.

Scholarship Information Request
133 Peachtree Street - N E
Atlanta, GA 30303

Phone: 404/652-4182

Scholarships: Variable

Max. Amount: Variable

Deadline: Variable

Contact: Scholarship Coordinator

Requirements: Application, Transcripts,
Financial need statement,
Proof of residency

Scholarship Description: Annual scholarships for graduating high school seniors who are children of Georgia-Pacific employees. These scholarships are administered in conjunction with the National Merit Scholarship Program and support the students' educational advancement at public and private schools. Selection is based on academic achievement, moral character, and financial need. Due date, award amount, and number of awards vary. More information is available by contacting the foundation or visiting the following online Internet address: http://www.gp.com/csrr/community/foundation.html

Golden Gate Restaurant Association

Scholarship Information Request
720 Market Street
San Francisco, CA 94102

Phone: 415/781-5348

\# Scholarships: Variable

Max. Amount: $5,000

Deadline: April 30

Contact: Scholarship Coordinator

Requirements: Application, Interview,
GPA, Recommendations

Scholarship Description: This award is provided by an association in the San Francisco Bay Area, representing restaurant owners and operators, to assist individuals committed to pursuing a career in the hospitality industry. Students who are California residents, who have graduated or are due to graduate within six months, and who have been accepted into a college level foodservice program are eligible to apply. Applicants must meet minimum grade and other criteria. Additional information on scholarship eligibility and application processes are specified at: http://www.ggra.org/productlist.asp?menuid=1247&submenuid=1789&CategoryID=4662

 # Goldman, Sachs, & Co.

Society of Women Engineers
Scholarship Selection Committee
120 Wall Street230 East Ohio St. Suite 400
Chicago, IL 60611-3265

Phone: 212/509/9577

\# Scholarships: 4

Max. Amount: $2,000

Deadline: May 15

Contact: Scholarship Coordinator

Requirements: Application, transcripts, 2 recommendation letters, ABET college acceptance

Scholarship Description: This scholarship is one of several granted by the Society of Women Engineers. For all scholarships, applicants must be women and Juniors or Seniors in High School with a minimum of a 3.5 GPA. Applicants must study engineering or computer science at an ABET/CSAB-accredited or SWE-approved institution. Recipients must be in a position to accept the scholarship in the school year for which it is granted. U.S. citizenship or permanent residence status is required, and applicants must not be receiving full educational funding from another organization; for example, an employer or the armed services. Additional scholarship information and application forms are available online at the following Internet address: http://www.swe.org/stellent/idcplg?IdcService=SS_GET_PAGE&nodeId=9&ssSourceNodeId=119

Harry S. Truman Scholarship Foundation

Scholarship Information Request
712 Jackson Place NW
Washington, DC 20006

Phone: 202/395-4831

Scholarships: Variable

Max. Amount: $30,000

Deadline: February

Contact: Scholarship Administrator

Requirements: Essay, Proof of residency, Reference letter, Application, Transcripts

Scholarship Description: Open to students who are U.S. citizens. These are merit-based scholarships awarded to Junior-level students at 4-year colleges and universities and/or Sophomore-level students at 2-year colleges who have outstanding leadership qualities, and who in the top 25% of their class. Applicants must intend to continue with graduate studies towards a career in public service (all fields are eligible if they are applied to public service careers). Additional information may be found at http://www.truman.gov.

Hitachi Foundation

Yoshiyama Community Service Award
1215 17th Street, NW
Washington, DC 20036

Phone: 202/457-0588

Scholarships: Variable

Max. Amount: $5,000

Deadline: Variable

Contact: Scholarship Coordinator

Requirements: Application form, Reference letter

Scholarship Description: Annual awards for graduating high school seniors in the U.S. and territories engaged in extraordinary community service. Students must be nominated. Nominators may be teachers, school principals, community leaders, service providers, or members of the clergy. In addition, nominators must be affiliated with community organizations/associations, schools, or churches. Students (or their parents) may not nominate themselves. Nominees need not be college bound. The award is based on service rather than academics or activities. More information is available online at the following website: http://www.hitachifoundation.org/yoshiyama/

Horatio Alger Association Scholarship

Scholarship Information Request
99 Canal Center Plaza
Alexandria, VA 22314

Phone: 703/684-9445

\# Scholarships: Variable

Max. Amount: $20,000

Deadline: October 30

Contact: Scholarship Coordinator

Requirements: Application form

Scholarship Description: This scholarship is open to high school seniors pursuing a bachelors at an accredited college in the U.S. Eligibility criteria include financial need, academic achievement, and community service. Additional information is available at the following website: https://www.horatioalger.com/scholarships/index.cfm

Institute for Humane Studies

Humane Studies Fellowships
George Mason University
3301 N. Fairfax Dr., Ste. 440
Arlington, VA 22201-4432

Phone: 800/697-8799

\# Scholarships: Variable

Max. Amount: $12,000

Deadline: Variable

Contact: Competition Coordinator
Requirements: Standardized test scores
Application, Fee, Resume

Scholarship Description: Awards are offered to undergraduate, graduate, law, and professional students who study in the United States or abroad. Applicants must be full-time students interested in exploring the principles, practices, and institutions necessary to ensure a free society through their academic work. Entry applications may be submitted online at http://www.theihs.org/scholarships/id.775/default.asp. Submissions include a registration process, and awards are based on academic or professional performance, relevance of one's work to the advancement of a free society, and a candidate's potential for success.

Jeff Krosnoff Scholarship

Jeff Krosnoff Scholarship
P.O. Box 8585
La Crescenta, CA 91214-0585

Phone: Not provided

Scholarships: Varies

Max. Amount: $10,000

Deadline: Varies

Contact: Scholarship Coordinator

Requirements: Essay, Application form,
Transcripts

Scholarship Description: Awards are available to graduating seniors in California high schools who intend to enroll in a four-year college or university. Requirements include a minimum GPA of 3.0, a written essay, excellent academic record, diversity of interests and extracurricular involvement, community citizenship, writing skills, and potential for success. The scholarship is presented at the Toyota Grand Prix of Long Beach gala. Application forms are available online at: http://www.krosnoffscholarship.com/Scholarship.htm

Johnson and Wales University

Gaebe Eagle Scout Scholarship
Johnson and Wales University
#8 Abbott Park Place
Providence, RI 02903

Phone: 800/342-5598

Scholarships: Varies

Max. Amount: $1,000

Deadline: February 1

Contact: Scholarship Coordinator

Requirements: Application, Transcripts,
Copy of Eagle Scout Certificate

Scholarship Description: All freshmen who have been accepted at Johnson and Wales University who have earned their Eagle Scout Award from the Boy Scouts of America may apply to receive the $1,000 award. Due date and number of awards varies. Scholarship applications are available via the Internet at: http://www.jwu.edu/admiss/pdf/sch_scout.pdf

KFC Colonel's Scholars Program

KFC Colonel's Scholarship
1900 Colonel Sanders Lane
Louisville, KY 40213

Phone: 866/532-7240

\# Scholarships: Varies

Max. Amount: $20,000

Deadline: February 16

Contact: Director of Admissions

Requirements: Essay, Transcripts,
Recommendation Letter,
Photograph

Scholarship Description: Available to high school seniors with an entrepreneurial drive, strong perseverance, and financial need who plan to attend a public in-state college or university for the undergraduate degree. Requirements include a minimum 2.75 GPA, and U.S. citizenship or permanent resident status. Details can be obtained from http://www.kfcscholars.org/

 # Leopold Schepp Foundation

Scholarship Information Request
551 Fifth Avenue - Suite 3000
New York, NY 10176

Phone: 212/692-0191

\# Scholarships: 200

Max. Amount: $8,500

Deadline: 30 November

Contact: Executive Secretary

Requirements: Interview, Application,
Financial need statement,
Transcripts

Scholarship Description: Approximately 200 awards are available each year to full-time undergraduate and graduate students enrolled at accredited colleges and universities. Character references are required and school and college evaluations are taken into account. Additional considerations include academic ability and financial need. Applicant must be U.S citizens or permanent residents. Age limits exist for first time applicants: undergraduates must be under 30 years old; graduates must be under 40 years old. No age limit exists for post-doctorate students. Graduates with only their dissertation left will not be considered. Applicants must attend an interview in New York City. Contact the foundation between 1 June and no later than 30 November for information and guidelines, or visit the organization's website at: http://www.scheppfoundation.org/applying.html

 # Lowe's Scholarship

Scholarship Progam Administrators Inc.
200 Crutchfield Avenue
Nashville, TN 37210

Phone: 615/320-3149

\# Scholarships: 300+

Max. Amount: $15,000

Deadline: March 1

Contact: Scholarship Coordinator

Requirements: Application

Scholarship Description: Lowe's scholarships are awarded to high school seniors planning to attend any two or four year college or university within the U.S. Annually, 336 scholarships nation-wide are awarded at $1,000, 21 regionally at $5,000, and one $15,000 grand prize winner. Application information can be obtained online through the Lowe's corporate website at http://www.lowes.com/lowes/lkn?action=pg&p=Scholarship/lowesfoundation_120606.html

 # Mahatma Rice Scholarship Program

Mahatma Rice Scholarship Program
PO Box 2636
Houston, TX 77252

Phone: 800/226-9522

\# Scholarships: 5

Max. Amount: $2,000

Deadline: None

Contact: Scholarship Coordinator

Requirements: Application, Essay

Scholarship Description: The Mahatma Rice Scholarship is awarded to high school seniors attending schools in Orange County or the Los Angeles area, New York, New Jersey, Miami, Chicago, or the San Francisco/San Jose metropolitan area. Submission entries must include an application and an essay on personal challenges anticipated in college. Applications may be submitted online at http://www.mahatmarice.com/scholarship

Most Valuable Student Competition

Elks National Foundation
2750 N. Lakeview Avenue
Chicago, IL 60614-2256

Phone: 773/755-4732

\# Scholarships: 500

Max. Amount: $15,000

Deadline: January 11

Contact: Scholarship Coordinator

Requirements: Application, Transcripts

Scholarship Description: The Most Valuable Student Competition is open to high school seniors who are U.S. citizens. Applicants must reside within the jurisdiction of a local Elks Lodge. Criteria are based on scholarship, leadership, and financial need. Applicants must pursue a four-year degree on a full-time basis (minimum of 12 semester hours) at a U.S. college or university. Applicants need not be related to a member of the Elks. Male and female students compete separately. Visit the Elk's website for more information and application forms at: http://www.elks.org/enf/scholars/mvs.cfm

National Association of Secondary School Principals

National Honor Society Scholarships
1904 Association Drive
Reston, VA 20191

Phone: 703/860-0200

\# Scholarships: Varies

Max. Amount: Varies

Deadline: Varies

Contact: Nat'l Honor Society Advisor

Requirements: Reference letter, SAT/ACT, Transcripts, PSAT/NMSQT

Scholarship Description: Recipients must be National Honor Society members. Each participating chapter nominates high school seniors, who display good moral character, leadership ability, and service to others. Scholarship may be used at accredited colleges, junior colleges or universities in the USA. State, regional, and national awards are granted each year. Contact local chapter or submit written request for guidelines and application forms. Candidates can also find out more about these scholarship awards online at the following website: http://www.principals.org/s_nassp/sec.asp?CID=571&DID=48231

National Peace Essay Contest

United States Institute of Peace
1200 17th Street NW, Suite 200
Washington, DC 20036-3011

Phone: 202/457-1700

\# Scholarships: Varies

Max. Amount: $10,000

Deadline: February 1

Contact: Contest Coordinator

Requirements: Four Copies of Essay,
      Online registration form

Scholarship Description: This award is open to students in the ninth grade through twelfth grade who attend public, private, parochial, or correspondence school programs in the U.S. The essay contest is intended to promote discussion among high school students, teachers, and national leaders about international peace and conflict resolution today and in the future. Essay submissions must be no more than 1,500 words. A local sponsor or contest coordinator is required who will review essays and act as liaison with the Institute. Additional guidelines may be found at http://www.usip.org/ed/npec/

 # National Security Education Program

NSEP David L. Boren Scholarship
Institute of International Education
1400 K Street, NW, 6th Floor
Washington, DC 20005-2403

Phone: 800/618-6737

\# Scholarships: Varies

Max. Amount: Varies

Deadline: Varies

Contact: Scholarship Committee

Requirements: Application, Transcripts,
      Two Letters of Reference
      Study Abroad Proposal

Scholarship Description: NSEP offers undergraduate students the opportunity to study abroad in regions critical to U.S. national security interests, including Africa, Asia, Central and Easter Europe, Eurasia, Latin America, the Caribbean, and the Middle East. Study of a foreign language appropriate to the identified country is a requirement. An NSEP requirement also stipulates that award recipients work in the Departments of Defense, Homeland Security, State, or Intelligence Community. All applications must be submitted online at this address: http://www.iie.org/programs/nsep/undergraduate/default.htm

NetAid Global Action Award

NetAid
75 Broad Street, Suite 2410
New York, NY 10004

Phone: 212/537-0500

\# Scholarships: Varies

Max. Amount: $5,000

Deadline: 15 December

Contact: Program Coordinator

Requirements: Application

Scholarship Description: This award honors high school students who have made significant contributions to the fight against global poverty, preventing HIV/AIDS, alleviating hunger, and improving access to education. Students must have organized and led an innovative project that directly impacted people living in poor countries and/or raised awareness about global poverty and related issues. Applicants must reside in the U.S. Submissions must include a personal statement and letter of reference. Students may learn more about this award at: http://www.netaid.org/global_action_awards/

Outstanding Students of America Scholarship

Outstanding Students of America
3047 Sagefield Road
Tuscaloosa, AL 35405

Phone: 205/344-6322

\# Scholarships: Varies

Max. Amount: $1,000

Deadline: October 10

Contact: Scholarship Committee

Requirements: Application, Biography, Essay

Scholarship Description: This scholarship is available to current high school seniors who have attained a minimum GPA of 3.0. Candidates must be able to demonstrate outstanding commitment to the community and school activities. A 250-word essay is required highlighting accomplishments and reasons why the applicant deserves the scholarship. Applications must be signed by the student and a teacher. Applications may be obtained online at http://www.outstandingstudentsofamerica.com/

# peermusic Latin Scholarship

BMI Foundation, Inc.
Ralph N. Jackson, President
320 W. 57th St.
New York, NY 10019

Phone: Not provided

\# Scholarships: 1

Max. Amount: $5,000

Deadline: January 26

Contact: Scholarship Coordinator

Requirements: Application form

Scholarship Description: The peermusic Latin Scholarship is available to songwriters between the ages of 16 and 24 who are students at colleges in the United States or Puerto Rico. Individuals must submit an original recording of a song or instrumental work in any Latin genre to be eligible for this scholarship award. Applications may be obtained online from http://www.bmifoundation.org/pages/peermusic.asp

Pinnacle Peak Solutions Achievement Award

Dave Fenstermaker
PO Box 11870
Glendale, AZ 85318

Phone: 800/762-7101

\# Scholarships: 1

Max. Amount: $500

Deadline: 30 June

Contact: Scholarship Coordinator

Requirements: Essay, Application form,
Transcripts

Scholarship Description: Pinnacle Peak Solutions is the owner and operator of http://www.scholarships101.com. It provides an annual award for undergraduate students who are U.S. citizens. This award recognizes not only academic excellence, but also the student who is self-motivated and a forward thinker. The organization is interested in fostering excellence within the United States and cultivating leaders who can provide leadership and vision. An essay is usually required.

Quill and Scroll International Writing-Photo Contest

Scholarship Information Request
U of IA School of Journalism
100 Adler Journalism Bldg. E 346
Iowa City, IA 52242

Phone: 319/335-3457

\# Scholarships: Varies

Max. Amount: Varies

Deadline: February 5

Contact: Scholarship Coordinator

Requirements: Portfolio, Sample works

Scholarship Description: Annual competition for all high school students. Each school may submit four entries in each of the following categories: Editorial, Editorial Cartoon, In-Depth Reporting (Individual & Team), News Story, Feature Story, Sports Story, Advertisement, and Photography (News/Feature and Sports), General Columns, and Review Columns. A $2 entry fee must accompany each entry. Contest rules are sent in late December to all schools on Quill and Scroll's mailing list. Guidelines and an entry form also appear in the December/January issue of Quill and Scroll magazine and on the following website: http://www.uiowa.edu/~quill-sc/Contests/contests.html. National Winners will be notified by mail through their advisers and receive the Gold Key Award, and be listed in the April/May issue of Quill and Scroll. Amount and number of awards vary.

Quill and Scroll Yearbook Excellence Contest

Scholarship Information Request
U of IA School of Journalism
100 Adler Journalism Bldg. E 346
Iowa City, IA 52242

Phone: 319/335-3457

\# Scholarships: Varies

Max. Amount: Varies

Deadline: 1 November

Contact: Scholarship Coordinator

Requirements: Application

Scholarship Description: Annual competition open to all Quill and Scroll charter high schools. Member schools may submit entries in 12 divisions: Theme Development, Student Life, Academics, Clubs or Organizations, Sports, People, Advertising, Sports Action Photo, Academic Photo, Feature Photo, Graphics and Index. Each school is limited to four entries per division except the Theme Development division which allows only 1 entry. A $2 fee per entry is required. Contest rules are sent (in late August) to all Quill and Scroll member schools. Guidelines and an entry form also appear in the April/May issue of Quill and Scroll magazine. National winners will be notified by mail through their advisers and receive the Gold Key Award, and be listed in the February/March issue of Quill and Scroll. Amount and number of awards vary. More information available at: http://www.uiowa.edu/~quill-sc/Contests/contests.html.

Ronald McDonald House Charities National Scholarship

Ronald McDonald House Charities
One Kroc Drive
Oak Brook, IL 60523

Phone: 630/623-7048

\# Scholarships: Varies

Max. Amount: Varies

Deadline: Varies

Contact: Scholarship Coordinator

Requirements: Reference letter, Transcripts, Resume, Application

Scholarship Description: The Ronald McDonald House Charities National Scholarship is award to high school seniors from communities that face limited access to educational and career opportunities. Applicants must be planning to attend a two- or four-year college or university with a full course of study and reside in a participating local Ronald McDonald House Charities Chapter's geographic area. Details and application forms may be obtained online at: http://www.rmhc.org/rmhc/index/programs/rmhc_scholarship_program.html

 # Rotary International Foundation

Academic & Multi-Year Ambassadorial
1 Rotary Center - 1560 Sherman Avenue
Evanston, IL 60201

Phone: 708/866-3000

\# Scholarships: Varies

Max. Amount: $23,000

Deadline: October 1

Contact: Scholarship Coordinator

Requirements: Reference letter, Resume, Essay, Application, Transcripts

Scholarship Description: This organization sponsors several types of scholarships for undergraduate and graduate students as well as for qualified professionals pursuing vocational studies. Recipients must be citizens of a country with a Rotary club. As ambassadors of goodwill, scholars must complete a language ability form and give presentations to Rotary clubs and other groups. Applications are processed through the local Rotary club. Information and applications are available at: http://www.rotary.org/foundation/educational/amb_scho/index.html

Sand Hill Scholars Program

Silicon Valley Community Foundation
60 South Market Street, Suite 100
San Jose, CA 95113-2336

Phone: 408/278-2200

\# Scholarships: 5

Max. Amount: $1,000

Deadline: March 7

Contact: Scholarship Coordinator

Requirements: Application, U.S. Citizen

Scholarship Description: The Sand Hill Scholars Program is available to graduating seniors at a California high school in San Mateo County or northern Santa Clara County (Daly City through Mountain View), or a current college student who graduated from a high school in Santa Clara or San Mateo County. Students must be graduates of Ravenswood City School District. Preference is given to students who have demonstrated motivation and leadership, who have overcome hardships to remain in school, or who have been involved in educational, job-related, or community activities outside the school environment. Additional information is available at: http://www.siliconvalleycf.org/grants_studentsTeachers_SCHOL.html#sc7

 # Scholastic Art and Writing Award

Alliance for Young Artists & Writers
557 Broadway
New York, NY 10012

Phone: 212/389-6100

Fax: 212/389-3939

\# Scholarships: Varies

Max. Amount: Varies

Deadline: Varies

Contact: Program Coordinator

Requirements: Application form,
Portfolio/sample works

Scholarship Description: The Scholastic Art and Writing Awards offer early recognition of creative teenagers and scholarship opportunities for graduating high school seniors. The purpose of the awards is to inspire the next generation of artists and writers. Annual awards are granted for students in the 7th through the 12th grade. An application and a portfolio must be submitted for an initial regional competition. More information is available online at: http://www.scholastic.com/artandwritingawards/enter.htm#about

Servant Leadership Essay Contest

Studentslead.net
4078 Morning Glory R. #5915
Colorado Springs, CO 80920

Phone: Not provided

\# Scholarships: Varies

Max. Amount: $5,000

Deadline: Varies

Contact: Award Coordinator

Requirements: Essay, Application

Scholarship Description: The Servant Leadership Essay Contest is available to undergraduate students enrolled in accredited four-year degree programs and high school seniors who plan to attend four-year colleges or universities. Candidates must have a minimum 3.0 GPA and be a U.S. citizen. Applicants must also submit an essay of 400-600 words answering the following question: "What does servant leadership mean to you, and how can you practice servant leadership in your college community?" This award is a cash grant. More information available at: http://www.studentslead.net/servantleadershipessay.html

Siemens Scholarship Competition

The College Board
Siemens Scholarship Program
45 Columbus Avenue
New York, NY 10023

Phone: 800/626-9795 x 5849/5930

\# Scholarships: Varies

Max. Amount: $100,000

Deadline: October 1

Contact: Scholarship Coordinator

Requirements: Application, Abstract,
Research Project

Scholarship Description: The Siemens Competition is comprised of an individual competition and a team competition. The individual competition is open to high school seniors. The team competition consists of two to three members from any level in high school. Individual and team entries receive separate awards. Contestants must submit a research project in science, mathematics, engineering, technology, or any combination of these disciplines. U.S. citizenship or permanent residency is required. Additional information and application available at: http://www.collegeboard.com/student/pay/scholarships-and-aid/23619.html

Thomas H. and Sarah Jane McIntosh Fund

The Pittsburgh Foundation
Five PPG Place, Suite 250
Pittsburgh, Pennsylvania 15222-5414

Phone: 412/394-2649

Scholarships: 3

Max. Amount: $15,000+

Deadline: Varies

Contact: Deborah Turner

Requirements: Essay, Transcripts, Letter of
reference, Application

Scholarship Description: The Thomas H. and Sarah Jane McIntosh Fund was established to provide assistance to students who have chosen a college major in writing, English, history, or political science at the University of Pittsburgh. Applicants must be fulltime students, have a minimum GPA of 3.0, and demonstrate financial need. An essay must be included that discusses the student's future goals and how their current field of study will help achieve these goals. Scholarship applications are available online at the following Internet address: http://www.pittsburghfoundation.org/Images/McIntoshApplication1.pdf

The Jackie Robinson Scholarship

The Jackie Robinson Foundation
National Headquarters
3 West 35th Street
New York, NY 10001-2204

Phone: 212/290-8600

Scholarships: Varies

Max. Amount: Varies

Deadline: Varies

Contact: Scholarship Coordinator

Requirements: Transcripts, Application,
SAT/ACT scores

Scholarship Description: Through its Education and Leadership Development Program, the Jackie Robinson Foundation provides scholarships to underserved high school students showing leadership potential and demonstrating financial need. Students must enroll at an accredited four-year college or university of their choice. Applicants must also be U.S. citizens. Additional information is available at: http://www.jackierobinson.org/apply/

U.S. Air Force ROTC

College Scholarship Program
HQ Air Force ROTC
551 E Maxwell Blvd
Maxwell AFB, AL 36112

Phone: 866/423-7682

Scholarships: Varies

Max. Amount: Varies

Deadline: December 1

Contact: Scholarship Coordinator

Requirements: Interview, SAT/ACT, Reference letter, Transcripts, Application, Medical exam, Admission letter

Scholarship Description: This award is available to high school students who are U.S. citizens and attend a college with an AFROTC program. Applicants must meet medical exam requirements. In addition, awards are based on SAT, ACT, GPA, class ranking, personal interviews, recommendations and extracurricular activities (not financial need). Academic major is also a consideration. Amount, number of awards, and lengths of awards vary by award type. Additional information may be obtained at: http://www.afrotc.com/scholarships/

Veterans of Foreign Wars

Voice of Democracy Scholarship
VFW National Headquarters
406 W 34th Street
Kansas City, MO 64111

Phone: 816/968-1117

Scholarships: Varies

Max. Amount: $30,000

Deadline: November 1

Contact: Director

Requirements: Audio Essay, Application

Scholarship Description: the Voice of Democracy scholarship program is an audio-essay contest for high school students in grades 9-12. Departmental winners also receive an all-expenses paid trip to Washington D. C. funded by Target. This program is sponsored by the National Association of Secondary School Principles and is designed to foster patriotism. Students voice their opinions in a three to five minute essay based on an annual theme. Recordings are submitted to a local Veterans of Foreign Wars Post. More information can be found at: http://www.vfw.org/index.cfm?fa=cmty.leveld&did=150

Wal-Mart Foundation

Wal-Mart Community Scholarships
702 SW 8th Street
Bentonville, AR 72716

Phone: 510/273-6850

\# Scholarships: Varies

Max Amount: $1,000

Deadline: Varies

Contact: Scholarship Coordinator

Requirements: Reference letter, Transcript
SAT/ACT, Resume, Essay,
Financial need statement

Scholarship Description: Wal-Mart scholarships are granted to high school seniors in communities serviced by a Wal-Mart store. These awards are based on academic merit, financial need, and school or work activities. The scholarship program is handled locally. Each store includes all high schools in its advertising area and awards one non-renewable scholarship. Applicants must have a 2.5 GPA. Applications are available starting in December and may be obtained from this website: http://www.wlamartfoundation.org.

Xavier University Scholarships

Xavier University Scholarships
3800 Victory Parkway
Cincinnati, OH 45207

Phone: 513/745-3142

\# Scholarships: Varies

Max. Amount: Varies

Deadline: December 1

Contact: Scholarship Coordinator

Requirements: Application, Admission

Scholarship Description: Xavier University Scholarships are annual awards. Applicants must be approved for admission to Xavier University. Scholarships are offered under many categories, including: academic, service, fine arts, alumni scholarships, minority scholarships, special categories, athletic, ROTC, state-sponsored. Some scholarships may be renewable for up to four years if full-time status is maintained along with specific GPA requirements. More information is available at the university's website address: http://www.xavier.edu/financial-aid/undergraduate-aid/scholarships.cfm

Youth Hall of Fame Scholarship Program

Youth Focus, Inc.
1620 Fruitdale Avenue
San Jose, CA 95128

Phone: 408/298-2644

Scholarships: Varies

Max. Amount: Varies

Deadline: Varies

Contact: Scholarship Coordinator

Requirements: Application, Essay, Resume

Scholarship Description: This scholarship is for graduating high school students residing in the Santa Clara County, California area. The program honors young people of merit for outstanding accomplishment in the areas of sports, community service, religion, vocational arts, visual arts, science, volunteerism, agriculture, heroism, youth leadership, youth in government and other meaningful categories. Award amounts may vary annually. Additional information may be obtained from the organization's website at http://www.youth-focus.org.

 # Zeta Tau Alpha Scholarships

Scholarship Information Request
3330 Founders Road
Indianapolis, IN 46268

Phone: 317/872-0540

Scholarships: Varies

Max. Amount: $1,000+

Deadline: March 1

Contact: Scholarship Coordinator

Requirements: Application, Membership

Scholarship Description: This foundation provides scholarships to undergraduate and graduates who are members of Zeta Tau Alpha. Awards are given on local, state and national levels ranging from $300 to over $1,000. Additional information can be obtained through the organization's website at http://www.zetataualpha.org/content/achievement/programs.asp

APPENDIX B

ACADEMIC
HIGH ACHIEVER
SCHOLARSHIP

APPLICATION

The

Academic High Achiever Scholarship

Award Application

The Academic High Achiever Scholarship Fund awards scholarships to outstanding high school students demonstrating exceptional achievement and excellence in all facets of their lives. Applicants are judged on the significance, breadth, and depth of their contributions and performance in the areas of academics, leadership, extracurricular activities, and community service as well as on their personal excellence and good character. All decisions are final. Stipends are to be used towards educational costs at an accredited four-year university or college. To be eligible, applicants must indicate definite plans to matriculate into a university during fall of the current school year.

Instructions

Adhere to the following directions carefully in completing the application:

- Please type--pencil or handwritten applications will not be accepted.
- Sign and date the completed application form.
- Use extra paper as necessary in listing honors, awards, and activities.
- Official high school transcripts must be submitted with each application.
- Obtain original letters of recommendation from the following:

    • A school teacher or administrator
    • A community, civic, or religious leader

- Submit a passport-sized photograph with the application form.
- Return the completed form no later than May 15 of the current year to:

    Academic High Achiever Scholarship Fund

Academic High Achiever Scholarship

Student Application

NAME_____

            Last   *First*   *Middle*

ADDRESS_____

           Street   *Apt #*

CITY_____STATE_____ZIP_____

PHONE_____DATE OF BIRTH_____ CHECK ONE (optional): ☐ Male ☐ Female

                                 Month/day/year

YEAR IN SCHOOL_____CURRENT HIGH SCHOOL ATTENDING_____

HIGH SCHOOL ADDRESS_____

CITY_____STATE_____ZIP_____

DATE OF ENTRANCE / PERIOD ATTENDED_____

CUMULATIVE GPA_____ # STUDENTS IN CLASS _____ RANK IN CLASS _____

SAT SCORE: Verbal_____ Math_____ ACT SCORE: _____

PLEASE LIST COLLEGES TO WHICH YOU HAVE APPLIED:

College/University:	Accepted	Will attend
_____	☐ Yes ☐ No	☐ Yes ☐ No
_____	☐ Yes ☐ No	☐ Yes ☐ No
_____	☐ Yes ☐ No	☐ Yes ☐ No

EMPLOYMENT HISTORY (last 3 years):

Employer	Position	Length of Employment	Hours/week

✐ What are your college career plans and future goals in life?

✐ Please list all honors, awards, scholarships, and achievements received in the last four years. Include year in school.

✐ Please list your scholastic activities, including leadership positions.

✐ Please list community activities or service in which you have been involved. Include year in school and any leadership positions held.

✐ In your opinion, what has been your most meaningful contribution to your home, school, and/or community. Why?

✐ To which personal characteristic(s) do you attribute your high school successes and experiences?

✐ Please record here any additional information which you feel will assist in assessing your qualifications for this award:

I certify that the information and references documented herein are truthful, original, and accurate. I understand that this application will become the property of the Academic High Achiever Scholarship Fund and hereby waive all claims in connection with its use for publicity and promotional purposes.

SIGNATURE_____DATE_____

Note: All applications should be accompanied by a $25 application processing fee.

BIOGRAPHIES

S.Y. Koot is the mother of four college graduates, a homemaker, and a community activist. She is a recipient of the Manuel Moreno Sr. Memorial Award from Youth Focus Inc. for her contributions to the welfare of youth and has also received her city's Citizen of the Year Award. S.Y. Koot founded of the Academic High Achiever Scholarship and is actively involved as a district leader in the Boy Scouts of America, where she has earned numerous accolades, including the Silver Beaver Award for meritorious service to youth. She has been a missionary in Asia and enjoys helping young people prepare for college scholarships.

Arthur L. Jue is a Director of Global Organization and Talent Development for Oracle. He has had extensive managerial experience at companies such as IBM and Hyperion and serves on the board of directors for educational, non-profit, and financial services organizations. Arthur has an MBA and Doctorate in Leadership, serves on the University of Phoenix faculty, is chair of Global Leadership for the International Leadership Association, and has been a missionary in New Zealand. Dr. Jue has also published widely on leadership and co-authored *Leadership Moments: Turning Points That Changed Lives and Organizations*.

Corine Neumiller is the mother of two children and works professionally as a registered clinical dietician. She enjoys researching cystic fibrosis as well as teaching nutrition at the University of Arizona Medical Center. Corine was a top scholar in high school, receiving numerous local, regional, and national honors. She earned a bachelors in Nutritional Science from SJSU and also attended BYU. In her spare time, Corine enjoys playing the violin as well as overseeing a regional Cub Scouting program for several hundred youth. She speaks fluent French and has served as a missionary in Belgium.